PENGUIN BOOKS

Sex is Perfectly Natural, But Not Naturally Perfect

Sue Johanson is a registered nurse who travels
extensively to teach sex and sexuality to thousands
of students and adults every year. She hosts a
nationally syndicated radio program "The Sunday
Night Sex Show," in addition to two weekly TV
shows: "Talking Sex" and "Sex, Drugs and Rock
'n Roll." Her first book, *Talk Sex*, addresses questions from teenagers.

SEX IS

PERFECTLY

NATURAL

But Not

Naturally

Perfect

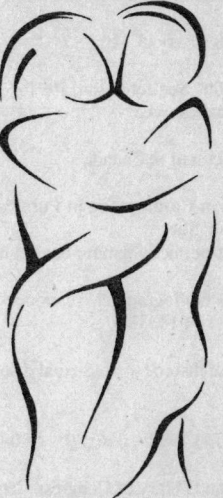

SUE JOHANSON

Penguin Books

PENGUIN BOOKS
Published by the Penguin Group
Penguin Books Canada Ltd, 10 Alcorn Avenue, Toronto, Ontario,
Canada M4V 3B2
Penguin Books Ltd, 27 Wrights Lane, London W8 5TZ, England
Penguin Books USA Inc., 375 Hudson Street, New York, New York
10014, U.S.A.
Penguin Books Australia Ltd, Ringwood, Victoria, Australia
Penguin Books (NZ) Ltd, 182-90 Wairau Road, Auckland 10, New
Zealand

Penguin Books Ltd, Registered Offices: Harmondsworth, Middlesex,
England

First Published in Viking by Penguin Books Canada Limited, 1991

Published in Penguin Books, 1992

10 9 8 7 6 5 4 3 2 1

Copyright© Sue Johanson, 1991
All rights reserved

Manufactured in Canada

Canadian Cataloguing in Publication Data
Johanson, Sue
   Sex is perfectly natural but not naturally perfect

Includes bibliographical references.
ISBN 0-14-013931-1

1. Sexual disorders. 2. Sexual disorders - Treatment.
I. Title

RC556.J63 1992   616.6'9   C90-095709-3

American Library of Congress Cataloguing in Publication Data
Available

Except in the United States of America, this book is sold subject to the
condition that it shall not, by way of trade or otherwise, be lent, re-
sold, hired out, or otherwise circulated without the publisher's prior
consent in any form of binding or cover than that in which it is published and without a similar condition including this condition being
imposed on the subsequent purchaser.

ACKNOWLEDGEMENTS

• • •

Most writers would have you believe they sweat blood writing their book. Not so for me, it has been pure joy. When I first mentioned writing another book, I had enthusiastic support from my publisher Penguin Books Canada. Laurel Bernard was given the task of coordinating the project. She knew the ropes, and she also knew how to get me mobilized when I bogged down. That was the best of all worlds for me. Then I got lucky again, Laurel found me an editor who is a gem. Jane Lind has a mind like a steel trap and the determination of a British bulldog, both of which I need to keep me on track, but there was always mutual admiration and respect for each other's abilities. We shared many good laughs and became friends along the way—neat lady and a pleasure to work with.

Full credit must go to my three children who constantly challenge me, keep me on my toes and in contact with reality, yet provide liberal doses of the "three big As"—acceptance, approval and appreciation. And thanks to my grandchildren who provide the total love and adoration that only grandchildren can give.

I would also really like to thank Dr. John Lamont, a gynaecologist and sex therapist at Hamilton Henderson Hospital, who graciously agreed to read the book for accuracy and provided insights that contributed a great deal to the context.

The manuscript was also read by Ann Barrett, Education Coordinator, Planned Parenthood of Toronto. She had many valuable points to offer. Contributions were also made by Dr. Michael Barrett, Department of Zoology, University of Toronto and chairperson of SIECCAN (Sex Information and Education Council of Canada). Sheila Brandick, a counsellor specializing in sex education and sexual therapy and a sessional lecturer for the faculties of Social Work and Medicine at the University of Saskatchewan, was kind enough to give the manuscript an expert read-over as well. Thank you all for your time and efforts.

With regard to the letters and confidences from listeners and viewers quoted in this book, none of them are verbatim or taken from individual letters—the letters I have used in the book are a compilation of the most common concerns and problems expressed in letters or in phone-counselling sessions.

I would like to thank all the listeners and viewers who have called me; and all those who have written describing their anguish, fear and sense of failure and inadequacy when their sex lives left much to be desired. They were the real inspiration for this book. I hope it is helpful for all of you.

Sue Johanson

FOREWORD

• • •

I would love to be able to say that I wrote this book for all the people who have concerns, anxieties or fears about sex, most of which are based on misinformation and misconceptions. To dispel these myths would be a lofty justification, but the reality is, I am writing it out of desperation.

As a sex educator-counsellor, I have a weekly phone-in radio show, a weekly one-hour TV show and a national TV show. Listeners and viewers can phone in and get answers to their questions about love, sex and relationships or explore their attitudes and values about sex.

And it blows my mind. The questions are basically the same today as they were five years ago when I first hit the media—what is normal, concerns about sexual performance and specific sexual dysfunctions—the reasons for their desperation and my frustration.

I also travel around teaching sexuality to large

groups of students, a total of 45,000 in 1990 alone. And here, again, the kids are preoccupied by basically the same questions and concerns that prevailed fifteen years ago when I started teaching sexuality.

In 1988 I wrote a book called *Talk Sex* to answer some of the more common questions kids ask about sex and sexuality. This book is for adults who are experiencing anxiety about their relationship or their sexual performance. It is based on my experience in counselling and my strong belief in the power of information combined with common sense.

I get letters from people who are not able to get through to the radio-TV shows. It is not uncommon for me to get a letter like this:

> *Dear Sue,*
> *Can you recommend any books that my partner and I can read to help solve our hang-ups? We are both shy, modest and inexperienced and have difficulty talking about sex. Perhaps a book we could share would help open it up a bit. There has got to be more to sex than this.*

To date, I have been unable to locate any one specific book like the one I visualized—one that focuses on essential aspects of any loving relationship and that also provides specific suggestions to help overcome the most common sexual dysfunctions.

As to how I would write the book, I decided I wanted it to be "an easy read," kinda fun, using some humour to diffuse the knee-jerk uptight reactions to discussing sex; and I wanted to write it in language and terminology that could be easily understood. As a registered nurse, it would probably have been safer for me to resort to "medicalese," which would not upset anybody. Now, I do not use gutter language or four-letter words, but I do use street language and everyday "slanguage."

I also decided I wanted the book to be a back-up for those already involved in sex therapy. So in this book I try to help you look at your sexual injunctions and expectations, decide if they are realistic and where they fit in your relationships and sexual activity. Because sex is so personal and private and intimate—not something we talk about easily—perhaps using this book will make it easier to work through your gut feelings of embarassment, guilt, shame, and the feelings that pleasurable sex must be immoral or sinful. That, combined with a great deal of pertinent sex education and information, can reduce the myths that hold you back in your sexual performance and pleasure.

The book is divided into two main parts: the first, "Back to Square One" is about the underlying issues in a sexual relationship and some practical suggestions; the second part, "When Your Body Lets You Down," focuses on problems you may encounter. The table of contents lists the chapter divisions in both main parts of the book so that you can easily refer to a given topic to answer specific questions.

A section on organizations that can offer help and an extensive topical reading list conclude the book. Most of the books listed are inexpensive paperbacks, some of them "pop psychology," but many will give you further insight into your particular area of concern.

This book is not designed to be a replacement for

individual or couple counselling. But there are people who may find that by reading it, they get back to basics once again and gain insight into the dynamics of their relationship. Other people may read this book and suddenly recognize and accept the fact that they do have a sexual problem, that help is available, and that it is relatively simple and non-threatening because now they have some idea of what to expect. Many sex therapists have told me they wish there was a book that they could recommend to their clients as an adjunct to therapy.

Here it is.

Another bonus: you just might get "turned on" while reading this book and instigate a little "action" on your own. Fantastic! Go for it!

Writing a book about sex is easier than discussing sex on radio or TV. There are things that are difficult to explain on radio without grossing everybody out. If a caller wants me to describe the "squeeze technique" for premature ejaculation, it is tricky to give the necessary details and be explicit enough so the procedure can be visualized without turning off the rest of the audience. Now I can just refer them to this book, which will give the necessary information and the encouragement to experiment.

A few explanations: I use the word "partner" instead of "husband" or "wife." Many couples are in stable, loving, sexual relationships, and are not necessarily married, and they, too, may have some sexual concerns. This book is written for singles, couples and married couples.

I am also very aware that my book refers to heterosexual couples, and I know that one in ten of our population is lesbian or homosexual, and they, too, have sexual and relationship problems. They are not being omitted, but as I was writing I would refer to "him and her" or "he and she." It became bogged down in a "cast of thousands" if I included "he and he" or "she and she." So I decided to use the male-female terminology and anyone in a same-sex relationship can substitute the appropriate language for themselves because, basically, the problems are much the same and the therapy similar. Please accept my apologies and know that you were not being ignored or passed over.

In addition, nobody is more aware than I: there are both male and female doctors, psychologists, sex therapists and counsellors. Generally I will refer to "the therapist" or "the doctor." But there are times when the client is a female, and I will refer to the therapist as "he," or vice versa. This is not sex-role stereotyping; it is in the interest of clarity and brevity.

Read this and other books alone, then aloud with your partner, discussing them as you go. That way you can both share and grow together.

I only hope it is "as good for you as it was for me."

CONTENTS

• • •

SEX IS
PERFECTLY
NATURAL

But Not

Naturally

Perfect

PART I
● ● ●
BACK TO
SQUARE ONE

CHAPTER 1

YOU ARE SEXUAL

• • •

SELF-IMAGE: LIKING YOU, LOVING YOU

You are sexual. You are a sexual human being from the moment you are born until the day you die. Your sense of yourself as a sexual person is closely tied in with your self-image—how you think about yourself and how you feel about yourself.

There are two distinct parts to your self-image. One is your self-concept: Who am I? What are my abilities? Am I okay? The other part of self-image is self-esteem: Am I a worthwhile person? Am I lovable? Am I capable and competent? How do you see me?

If we do not feel good about ourselves and our sexuality, and we don't think anybody would ever find us attractive and sexy, then we tend to settle for less than the very best. Because we don't feel we are as good as everybody else, we do not feel we are entitled to all we want in a good relationship: one that is warm, caring, committed, with good communication and intimacy. We are also reluctant to insist on good contraception and safer sex. In other words, we end up settling for less than we deserve, and our compromises do us in, in the end.

Our sexual self-image starts during earliest childhood. We allow babies to explore their toes and we even play "This Little Piggy Goes to Market" with them. But if they make a grab for their genitals, we promptly take their hand away and say, "Dirty, dirty, don't touch." Now, they know touching their genitals feels good and that mommy and daddy don't like it when they do it, so they learn to do it surreptitiously, in a hurry and with some guilt, shame, fear and embarrassment. As they grow older, they hear all the myths about masturbation: you will go bald or blind; you will hurt yourself or get an infection; you will wear it out; or you are homosexual if you "play with yourself."

Often when kids become teenagers and develop acne, they immediately blame masturbation. Their self-image is shattered because their secret is out; the whole world knows they have been doing it.

Because their self-image is wobbly at this time in their lives, they may not accept the fact that "zits" are not caused by "jerking off." Unless they make a conscious effort to get the facts, explore their attitudes and values and decide what is right for them, they may carry these inhibitions with them for life.

This only covers inhibitions about masturbation.

Think of all the other areas of our sexuality; for example, our body image. Very few of us are totally satisfied with our own body as it is. We are so conscious of our inadequacies: "thunder thighs," stretch marks, "cellulite city," big boobs or "terminal flats," tight buns or "being well hung." Few people, even in their prime, could make the centre-fold of *Playboy* or *Playgirl*, supposedly the epitome of sexual attractiveness. We ignore all our good points and focus on our perceived "imperfections." Too often, we convince ourselves that we do not deserve great sex or even good sex with a loving partner, because of our physical imperfections.

We also tend to believe everything we read, hear or see about sexual performance. So, a few years ago, when we heard that the ultimate sexual delight was for both partners to experience multiple, spontaneous, simultaneous orgasms every time they had sex, we set out to reach that ultimate ecstasy. This, of course, is totally unreal. But if you have a low self-image, that niggling doubt about simultaneous orgasm will always be there and you will wonder if you have failed as a lover.

Your partner may tell you "You are the greatest," and you may want to believe it. But if you pick up one negative message—"That was great honey, but next time let's try it with me on top"—you may immediately interpret that as "It could have been better if only. . . ." You may even cultivate the feeling of failure and blow it out of all proportion, so that it might cause performance anxiety that will persist for years.

In contrast, if you have a good self-image, you will feel you deserve the best and you can go out and get it. If you do get negative "vibes" from your partner and you have enough self-confidence, you can check it out and find out exactly what is going on. You might say something simple, such as "Hey dear, remember when you said it might be fun to try it with you on top? Sounds like great fun, you foxy lady, you. . . ." There's a wonderful expression for a good self-image like this—*chutzpah*.

With this response, you are making sure your partner is interpreting your message correctly. It takes guts to go back and open it up for discussion, and it takes sensitivity not to put your partner down when he or she makes a suggestion. It would be easier to let sleeping dogs lie. But, if you and your partner have established open, honest communications then it will not be threatening to go back and clarify the original statement. You may even expand on it and learn more about your partner and your relationship.

Everybody needs reassurance—and it's easy to give if you practise the "three As": acceptance, approval and appreciation. If you are able to say "I really like it when you . . .", the message gets through: "you are great and I really like you."

When you were newly in love, you gave your beloved plenty of positive strokes, and you both blossomed. Both you, your partner and your relationship can always thrive with positive reaffirmation. It is so easy, so painless and so effective.

Once you are aware of the chinks in the armour of your self-image, then you can go back and resolve them, one by one. Think of one negative thing about yourself. Let's say you are reluctant to take the initiative. (This could apply to both males and females.) Now, think of all the ways this holds you back. Do you really want to be able to make a move? What is stopping you? Probably, fear. What are you afraid of? What is the worst thing that could possibly happen if it did not work? Could it be fear of rejection? What is so bad about being rejected? Would it be the end of the world? At least you tried. In all probability, though, your partner would be impressed, curious and would think there was nothing to lose, and would either accept or make alternative suggestions.

There are a few books you can read to gain some insight and understanding into your self-image and how to improve it. *Intimate Connections* by Dr. David Burns is useful for both males and females. *Women and Self-Esteem* by Linda Tschirhart-Sanford and Mary Ellen Donovan takes it more from the female point of view.

Attitudes and values are acquired along with self-image in early childhood and must constantly be evaluated in light of new information and changing morality. This letter is a classic example:

Dear Sue,
I have been with my partner for over four years now. I love him and the sex is good. But I have never yet been able to reach orgasm. I get to a certain point, then I stop. Now Sue, don't tell me to learn to masturbate because I just can't do that.

Another example is from a young male:

Dear Sue,
For some reason, I just can't "go down" on my girlfriend. I love it when she gives me oral sex, but I just can't bring myself to do it for her.

I do not want to go into all the possible reasons these people had for their particular "can'ts". But I want to focus on that operative word, because there wasn't any physical reason for it. What they are really saying is not "I can't" but "I won't." And they must take responsibility for the reason why they "will not" be involved in solitary masturbation or oral sex or whatever.

I am not saying that you have to do something whether you want to or not. If you are not comfortable with it, if it is repugnant to you, if you feel it is immoral, that is fine. But you can examine why it is so distasteful to you. Where did you get the idea that it is "gross"? Is that idea based on actual fact or on myth and misconception? Is it from a strong negative injunction from your parents, religion or friends? Or is it something you have a "block" about?

It is okay to have blocks—we all have them—just as long as we are aware of what they are and where we got them. Then we can choose whether we want to hold on to them, or whether we'd rather examine them in light of new, accurate information and maybe alter them, or let them go.

This is what's called personal growth. Sometimes it is hard work—you have to force yourself to do it. Sometimes it is frightening—these are all new ideas and you may want to retrench for a while to integrate your feelings into behaviour that is comfortable. Other times personal growth is exciting and you may just want to barrel ahead and make these challenging changes.

Be sure to pause and give yourself credit for making changes. This will strengthen your self-image. And it is important—actually essential—to share your new found sense of yourself with your partner. You have come a long way, baby. . . .

ATTITUDES AND VALUES: YOU ARE WHAT YOU ARE BECAUSE OF WHAT YOU WERE WHEN . . .

To understand where you are coming from right now, it is essential to go back and look at where you came from—your "family of origins"—because that is where you got your first messages about sex. These messages will continue to influence you, even control you, unless you are able to work your way through and discard ideas and concepts that are no longer valid.

Sounds like Psychology 101, but it is an essential process if you want to become comfortable and accepting of your sexuality and the sexuality of your partner, your children and those around you.

So let's take a few minutes and think about how your family reacted to the whole topic of sex and sexuality. What are your first recollections of sex? How was nudity handled? Were your parents comfortable if you accidentally saw one of them getting dressed or showering? Were they comfortable if you ran around nude as a toddler?

Could you ask innocent questions about sex: "How come he has a penis and I don't?" How about the more graphic questions such as "Mommy, how do you get a baby?"

Then move on and think about messages that you got about your body. If your parents discovered you examining your genitals in the bath tub, how did they react? Did they just let it go or were you told things like "Don't do that, you will hurt yourself," or "Don't touch, you'll get an infection"?

And what happened when you were caught "playing doctor"? If you are a male, would it have been any different if it had been your sister who was caught? This is important because males get different injunctions about sex than females do, and this strongly influences their attitudes towards themselves as sexual human beings and towards their partners.

Then there is the language of sex. As parents, we teach children the proper name for nose, not "shnoze," and eyes are not called "peepers." But when it comes to sexual organs, many parents are reluctant to use proper terminology. Instead they resort to slang or street language. So a penis is a "weenie" and breasts are referred to as your "chest," at best, or even "boobs" or "titties." Female genitals are generally referred to as "down there" which could mean anything south of the Canada-United States border.

If you, as a child, asked a specific question about sex, did you get a straight answer? Were you told: "I'll tell you when you are older. You don't need to know that just now." As a teenager, could you ask questions about birth control, homosexuality, masturbation, pregnancy or "Mom, does it hurt to have sex?"

As you grew older, other subtle messages included "sit with your knees together" (female) to "Don't stare at a girl's breasts" (male) and "hands off" for both sexes. As you matured, what other messages can you recall? How about "Girls don't smell very good when they have their period," to "If you pop a boner, hide it. Don't let anybody know you are horny."

By finding out what messages you were given when you were growing up, you can pinpoint where your attitudes come from. Perhaps your ideas started with your family's religion. You may have learned that masturbation is a sin and that virginity is essential before marriage (as exemplified by the "big white wedding"). Homosexuality is still seen as morally wrong by some religions. Others now say that homosexuality is not wrong, but acting on your homosexual tendencies is wrong. Society's attitudes towards these religious rules have definitely changed, some more than others, and we now accept behaviours that were unthinkable a number of years ago, for example, unmarried partners living together, choosing to have a baby without a partner, and divorce.

When you have some insight into your feelings about sex, take some time to get up-to-date, accurate information. Then evaluate your basic beliefs and translate your knowledge into attitudes, then on into practice. How is it going to apply to your life?

Don't try to do this overnight: you might just "throw out the baby with the bath water." Take time to explore and evaluate.

Another important consideration: If you are in a loving relationship, share your thoughts and information with your partner. Talk about it as you go along. Your partner may agree or disagree, and you may have to come to some compromise along the way. But it will be easier after some discussion, than if you make a complete about-face out of the clear blue sky and your partner begins to wonder if they know you any more.

Read on, we are on a roll here. . . .

SEX EDUCATION: WHERE DID YOU LEARN THAT?

Sex Education At Home

We are preoccupied with sex; in fact we are super-saturated with it. Sex is used to sell everything from deodorant to cars to oven cleaner.

Despite our preoccupation with sex, most of us have learned very little about it and many of us are uncomfortable talking about it to anybody, including our own loving partners. What's worse, as parents we are often nervous and embarrassed to talk to our own kids about sex. But it is essential that we give our children accurate, honest, up-to-date information because what they learn about sex at an early age will affect them throughout their lives, as this letter shows:

> Dear Sue,
> I remember as a kid finding a Playboy magazine and there was one picture of a female, legs akimbo, spreading her labia with her hands.
> I looked at that picture of her genitals, took a mirror and looked at mine. My mother caught me and nearly died. She said I was dirty and sick. To this day, I cannot look at or touch my genitals.

We teach our kids about their sexuality from the day they are born, from the way we touch their feet compared to the way we touch their genitals, to the way we react when we discover them "playing with themselves."

As parents, we become upset when we discover our kids "playing doctor" with their little friends. But it is so normal; all mammals "rehearse" sexual activity as they are growing up. Young monkeys playfully mount each other and practise making "all the right moves." They are learning social skills, courtship and mating rituals, so that when the time comes, they are capable and competent.

If they are isolated as young monkeys, they do not develop the social skills and retreat to a corner when in the presence of other monkeys. Without practice, their back legs are not strong enough to mount a female, nor do they know what to do when they get there. All mammals play at sex, with other animals, same sex, opposite sex, even with your foot if it is convenient.

But humans actively discourage their young from rehearsing. We expect humans to known by divine intuition how to do it right the very first time with no information, no instruction, simply "You'll know when the time comes." We add to the confusion when we tell females: "Your husband will teach you all you ever need to know." Is it any wonder that the old-fashioned honeymoon night has been such a horror show for many, many couples?

As parents today, we have an obligation to teach our kids about sex. In the process, I am convinced parents learn a great deal too. We cannot leave it up to the schools to teach sex; our kids deserve a combined education at home and school. Our kids also pick up their attitudes and values about sex from watching the way we show affection to our partners and listening to us as we discuss sexual issues.

It is much easier to provide knowledge if you start when your children are very young. Answering questions as they come up, in language they understand, giving "age appropriate" information. Don't worry, you cannot give too much. You will know when you have answered their questions and they have had enough. They simply "click off" and want to go out and play. All you have to say is: "Anytime you have questions, come and ask me." You have established yourself as approachable and they will be back.

As your kids approach adolescence, talk to them about things like body changes during puberty, and don't forget to talk about the feelings—attraction to somebody, feeling sexy, being in love. Talk about things like wet dreams. Both males and females have them, and both are convinced that they are oversexed and have too many hormones "oozing out of every pore." Teenage males feel that they have lost control. Females feel guilty, embarrassed and ashamed to be dreaming about sex and becoming aroused to the point of lubrication. "Nice girls" do not think about sex, and nice girls certainly do not dream about sex so they think. Wanna bet? Both males and females need to know that it is normal and natural and okay.

If you don't have the answer to a specific question, you can simply say, "You know what, I don't know about that and I am curious too. So I will find out and get back to you as soon as possible." Be sure to follow up on your promise.

If you are embarrassed talking about sex, admit it right away. You can say something like: "There is something we need to talk about, but I have been putting it off because I am embarrassed. But you need to know about sex, so if you can just hang in there with me, we will probably both learn a lot."

If you feel that you have pulled a real "boo-boo" and you don't like how it came out or if it was incorrect or sexist, no harm done. Just say, "Remember when we were talking about sex and I told you . . . well, I checked it out and I was wrong" or "I was thinking about it and I realized that I was being a real chauvinist and I want to correct that."

Talk about sex every time there is an opportunity—an article in the newspaper or a controversial hit song. Open it up for discussion. This does not mean that you treat your kids to a twenty-minute tirade about pre-marital sex, but ask how they feel about things. Then you listen, really listen to them. They are developing their theories right then and there. Don't jump in to correct them or impose your attitudes and values on them or put them on the defensive. Let them think it through and you will probably find that they are not "too far off base" as far as you are concerned.

If you don't agree, fine. You can say, "You know I never thought of it that way. You have some interesting points. There are a few things I am concerned about." Then outline your feelings and leave it open for discussion. This way, you are not imposing your "injunctions" on your kids, and they will be less inclined to rebel.

Buy them a book about sex for their birthday; they can keep it for referral when they have a question. Go to the library and pick up books about sex; leave them out on the coffee table for them to glance at. They will get hooked and read it, cover to cover.

Your kids are going to be exposed to sex on TV, in rock videos and afternoon soaps.

If they are home watching TV on a professional development day, afternoon soaps will treat them to one long series of torrid sexual scenarios.

And remember the furor about the "Venus Butterfly" referred to in a passionate scene in "L.A. Law"? *Playboy* published a three-page article summarizing this sexual manoeuver. Now, years later, I am still getting questions about it. It aroused a lot of curiosity, but it was a hoax.

You can censor your kids, but not what they watch. They'll see it somewhere. Instead, ask your kids how they feel when they see Madonna prancing around in a little bustier, singing "Like a Virgin." Again, really listen. Then you can say how and why that scene makes you feel uncomfortable. It is important to help your kids develop "media smarts," so they can analyse and be discerning, even critical.

You are teaching them to think for themselves, and that is exactly what you want them to do. They are not always going to agree with you. The main function of adolescence is to prepare for separation from hearth and home. One of the ways kids do this is to argue and debate, even rebel, to establish their own identity. They need to develop decision-making skills, and they cannot be expected to make logical, rational, appropriate decisions in a vacuum, if they do not have the necessary information on which they can base conclusions.

I say all this because raising kids can be one of the most enlightening phases of our lives. Children push us to learn, to explore, to experience all aspects of living, including our sexuality.

Sex Education in School

Although most parents strongly support sex education in schools, it is still controversial. Parents who oppose it are convinced that we are giving kids permission to "go right out and do it." They want their children to have the same attitudes and values that they themselves have. Others feel that sex information forces their children to "grow up too fast." They want their kids to stay young, innocent, naive and childlike.

Like it or not, kids are learning about sex from their friends. Much of that is myth and misinformation which could result in a serious situation. One common myth, "You can't get pregnant the first time you do it," has resulted in countless teen pregnancies. Our kids deserve better than that.

Recent studies by Dr. James Check at York University, Toronto, tell us that most kids are learning about sex from watching porno flicks on the VCR. They come home for lunch while parents are at work. They find some good porn tapes that have been stashed away, plug one in and watch women being brutalized, whipped and beaten, apparently enjoying frenzied, passionate orgasms. Seeing this, kids are convinced that this is the way it should be. This is what women like. So, is it any wonder, then, in a dating situation, if she says "no" to sex, he believes this is the normal pattern and that she really "wants it"? She may well become the victim of date rape because of this misinformation.

Sex education in schools generally begins in grade nine, focusing on sexually transmitted diseases (STDs) and birth control, with less attention on sexual feelings, love or relationships. It is taught primarily in physical education and health and is more detailed in grade ten. Unfortunately, most kids drop physical education in grade ten, so they may graduate with only the very basic information about sex.

While most school boards have a fairly comprehensive sex education program, many do not touch on the controversial issues such as masturbation, abortion and homosexuality. Some school principals are concerned about negative parental reaction, and for that reason may delete some important aspects. Not all teachers are comfortable teaching sex; still others have moral biases preventing them from teaching the topics adequately. Consequently, the course may be watered down to the basic "plumbing of sex," or what Dr. Sol Gordon, a well-known sex educator and author, calls "the relentless search for fallopian tubes."

AIDS triggered a concerted effort to inform kids about its transmission. Now schools are teaching kids about "retrovirus" and "seropositive" and "body fluids." Because this information has little or no meaning for kids, they ignore it. Very few educators talk about the risks of oral-genital sexual contact with an infected partner or about all the risks of anal intercourse. Yet a recent study from Queen's University of students from across Canada revealed that fifteen percent had been involved in anal sexual activity by the time they went to university. This is high-risk behaviour unless they are practising "safer sex." Even then, there is an element of risk.

As parents and as educators, we have a duty to teach our kids sexual survival skills, the most important of which is how to use a condom properly every time.

And we have to help them develop the communication skills to negotiate safer sex with a partner. To do this, our kids need to be able to talk amongst themselves, or they need to work in small groups to practise roles in different situations so they are familiar and comfortable with the words and phrases that would get their message across without it sounding negative, like a put-down or a rejection.

It is difficult to give your kids this help if you have never been comfortable talking to your partner about sex yourself. So, by reading this book, you can increase your knowledge and your comfort level with the topic. Then you can break down the barriers to learning about sex, to talking about sex and to enjoying your own sexuality.

CHAPTER 2

BARE ESSENTIALS

• • •

RELATIONSHIPS: ONE ON ONE

Most sexual problems, the ones that cause sexual dysfunctions, are basically relationship problems. Granted, there are other causes: physical abnormality, drugs, medications, surgery, aging, negative life experiences such as incest or sexual assault. But the most common underlying thread in most sexual dysfunctions is ongoing problems in the relationship between the two partners.

When you think back to the beginning of your relationship, when you were first "in love," the chemistry was there, the juices were flowing; it was mad, passionate love. You gazed adoringly into each other's eyes, oblivious to the rest of the world. You touched each

21

other continuously. There was total acceptance between you and your beloved, warts and all.

This was probably the one time in your life when you were the most open and honest about yourself and your feelings. You shared all your strengths and weaknesses, secure in the knowledge that there would be total acceptance. You were willing to risk, a little at a time in the beginning, but when each revelation was accepted, you moved on to more risky admissions: past loves, emotional hurts and personal failures. It really was a time of "true confessions." Your trust level was up.

This was also the time in your life when you intuitively practised empathic listening and communicating skills. You were a wonderful listener, totally absorbed in what your partner was saying, never questioning but reiterating their thoughts back to them.

There are many terms to describe this phase—love, lust, the "grand passion," but "limerance" is probably the best word to describe the state you were in. Limerance is a word I just picked up from another therapist—it seems to have lusty and starry-eyed glimmer of love in bloom all rolled up into the glow of new love.

Fortunately and unfortunately, limerance lasts only for about six months. I say fortunately because people just could not keep up that pace for a prolonged period of time. Sooner or later they have to get back to the real world out there and function. But unfortunately, when they do, most people put their empathic communication skills in storage.

Once that state of passionate love has simmered down, it settles into compassionate love—more subdued, stable, sensitive, aware and ongoing. You feel you really know your partner. You can almost anticipate exactly what he or she is thinking and what he or she is going to say next. So you stop really listening, and because you think you are boring each other, you stop really sharing.

So while compassionate love is comfortable like an old slipper, you might have to recharge it by re-establishing close intimate communications. Every couple creates unspoken rules that regulate their existence together. These rules often create more pain than pleasure and contribute to the dysfunction.

If you are genuinely determined to get more out of your relationship at this stage then you will have to retrieve the communication skills that you really do have, though they may be rusty from lack of use. For this reason, please be sure to read the section on "Communication" (see pages 31-40). Then reread it aloud with your partner and practise together. It works.

In any relationship, once the trust level is up and the communications are open and honest, a sense of intimacy can develop. Intimacy is that important sense of connectedness, of mutuality, of intense closeness with a partner. Unfortunately, in our language use of the word "intimacy" almost always involves sexuality. But in fact it is possible to have a very intimate, loving relationship with another person without sex being part of it.

Don't expect intimacy to stay the same at all times. Intimacy is never static in any relationship. A time of intense intimacy and feelings of "one-ness" is often followed by a period of backing off. This separation is essential because you also need a sense of autonomy, of being an individual, of being unique and not "joined at the hip." You require time to feel complete in yourself and to integrate with other people. Then and only then can you move once again into intimacy with your partner. Think of it as the "yin and yang" of relationship. It is normal and it is the only way the relationship will survive. If there is a healthy ebb and flow in the relationship, it will work very well.

Why Relationships Fall Apart

There are countless problems encountered in a relationship: money, job demands, household responsibilities, parents and in-laws, religion, children, outside interests, sports and hobbies, friends, the whole gamut. In the midst of all these pressures, often relationships start falling apart.

When we are very, very young, we developed in our heads an image, a "love map" of what we want in a love relationship. We then use this as a model of what we want in a partner. When our partner does not live up to our fantasies, we often feel disillusioned and dissatisfied. Then we accuse our partner of changing: "You are not the person I married." But in fact the partner has remained the same. We have not seen the real person because we were so caught up in our fantasy person.

If you have never learned communication skills, and have never learned problem-solving skills, then your relationship is bound to take a real battering. Fights and arguments break out and are never really settled. They are just temporarily stored away in a "scarbage bag" and every argument just adds a little bit more to the anger and resentment.

From here, it is easy to get into "dirty fighting," blaming, dredging, muckracking and what I call the "your mother wears army boots" syndrome. Nothing is resolved, and even after you make up, there is residual resentment, a sudden awareness of the widening gap between you and your partner. You may be concerned that you might never be able to pick up the pieces and get back on track again. This classic letter says it all:

> *Dear Sue,*
> *We have been married for five years. We have no children because I am not sure we are going to survive as a couple. I am starting to pull away, to make a life for myself apart from him. But that is not what I want, so I am thinking of leaving him. I still love him; we were so good together. But now it is the silent treatment with bursts of anger, pouting and me crying. Is there any way we can pull this together again, or should I just leave him? Please help us.*

There has been so much damage done to this relationship that it is in jeopardy. All is not lost, but they are going to need some good relationship counselling.

Power struggles often threaten a relationship and efforts to get the upper hand may occur when partners feel they are "low man on the totem pole," have no say in decision-making or feel used or manipulated. These feelings compound the anger and resentment, and in an effort to gain some sense of equality, one of the partners may resort to using sex as a way to even the score and gain control in at least one area of the relationship.

Women sometimes play psychological games in the struggle to gain some sense of power in a relationship that they are not finding egalitarian. During sex if she remains passive, "lies there like a plank," she may be saying, "You can do it, but I will be damned if I am going to make it pleasurable for you. And no way am I going to let you think you are a good lover. I am calling the shots here."

Males also play psychological games. He may withhold sex, implying: "You don't turn me on; you're not so hot," or "You will get sex when I am damn good and ready."

The problem is, if you play games like this, you may win the battle but lose the war. Leading sex therapists say there is no uninvolved partner in a sexual dysfunction.

A relationship also runs into problems if the partners are out of sync. He may want intimacy and she is out there doing her own thing. Then she wants to get close and he is off on a work tangent. This requires an in-depth discussion and compromises till both partners are in step again.

Problems escalate when the periods of intimacy become farther and farther apart. When both partners make their separate lives too comfortable, they effectively close each other out. Then the "urge to merge" is no longer there; they do not appear to miss the closeness, the sex drive dwindles and, once again, they will need to make a concerted effort to reconnect.

In a long-standing relationship, sex does not always rank first in the list of priorities. In a top-ten list of importance, sex may rate a six, after money, family, friends, leisure activities, work—then sex. In loving, committed relationships, if there are sexual problems this is not seen as "the end." But if the relationship is rocky and sex is not good, then the sexual problems assume monumental proportions.

If there is anxiety about the relationship, you may find yourself analysing every nuance (not always correctly). Don't jump to any premature conclusions while things are a bit dicey. You do not want to risk making the situation worse. It can really confuse your partner if you start modifying your behaviour according to wrong assumptions. You might get statements from your partner like "What is going on? I never know where you are coming from anymore." The truth is, neither do you.

It is better to be completely honest and quietly say, "You know what? I am just as bewildered as you are. Can we take some time, go back and clarify a few things, because I am scared it is going to get worse. I like 'us,' and I want our relationship to work."

You may continue to muddle through, hoping the problems will go away and things will be back to normal once the kids are back at school or the finances are okay. Well, they might, but more likely, the fighting will continue. There are usually too many unresolved conflicts in a relationship. Eventually your little problems may be so large that you or your partner want to give up in despair. One partner may decide to seek a better relationship or to pull away, withdraw, in preparation for getting out.

You may ask them, "Is everything okay?" and they say, "Sure, I'm just tired, that's all." Or, you may say, "I love you," and they tell you that they love you too, but something does not ring true.

To be honest there are so many old wounds in a relationship like this that it is going to take a concerted effort to get this show back on the road. At this point, you and your partner will probably need help to solve your problems.

Most couples would probably benefit from relationship counselling after one year of marriage or living together. Anytime you find yourself bogged down with unresolved conflict, get help—fast.

But before you go for counselling, it is important to be honest with yourself. If you have any suspicions that you are not really committed to making the relationship work—if you feel that you want out—then, please, arrange for a counselling session alone with the therapist. Indicate that you have real doubts that your relationship can be saved, because you are not sure that is what you really want. Then the therapist understands what is going on and can help you decide what it is that you really want. There is no sense going for counselling to save a relationship, if that is really not what you want. Once you are clear, then the therapist can work towards making the split as painless as possible.

For most couples, once the relationship is in trouble, the sexual activity is less frequent and less enjoyable until it grinds to a halt. But there are exceptions—I do know couples who simply do not work out together on a day-to-day basis, but their sex together is spectacular. This letter is an example:

Dear Sue,
My husband and I fought like tigers, non-stop,
screaming, yelling, bashing each other, walking out

*on each other, both of us having "torrid affairs," yet
we had fantastic sex right up till the day he moved
out. Even now, we still fight over custody and finan-
cial support. But every time he comes to town, we
have a real fantastic sexual romp, just like old times.
Do you think it will ever die out between us? My parents think we are both crazy. What do you think?*

My answer to this couple would be: Does it matter
what I think? It's what you think and feel that matters.
If it is acceptable to both of you and nobody else is
going to get hurt, then it is your decision. I would be
concerned what effect this is having on your children
(if they know). It might be very confusing and upsetting for them.

Putting It Back Together

Most couples who start working on their relationship begin to feel really intimate and close again. How
about a few suggestions to put a little spark back into
your sex life?

• **Be innovative.** Now, I am not talking another
black-lace nightie. Put a duvet down in front of a romantic fire in the fireplace or how about taking a
sleeping bag out on your private balcony and "fool
around" out there? Try doing it in front of a full-
length mirror or in the shower. You decide. How
about slowly, seductively, undressing each other, button by button, singing "I Wanna Kiss You All Over"?

How about a "nooner" or a "quickie" before the
kids come home from the movies? How about doing
some things that "nice girls" don't do. Amazing how

much fun you can have with a feather boa. Or, on her birthday, surprise her with a different present. Tie a big yellow ribbon around your penis and bounce in from the bathroom singing "Happy Birthday" and "Tie a Yellow Ribbon Around the Old Oak Tree."

• **Talk.** Tell your partner how good the sexual sensations feel to you: "I love to feel your penis inside me." You may have a little difficulty using street language, but try some of the less objectionable phrases; "I would like to screw you right into the mattress." It can trigger a whole new fantasy.

• **Be playful.** This is not "dead serious." Sex is fun and funny, so ham it up and be prepared to laugh. Write him a mash note, "Hurry home to your hot honey," and put it in his briefcase. I know a lady who set up her camera on time delay, arranged herself in a series of sexy poses, wearing black net stockings and high heels, in a satin peignoir with a bit of thigh showing, in a bubble bath, in the kitchen with only an apron on. Whenever he went out of town, she packed one picture on top of his pyjamas, and when he got home, he was practically kicking the door down. How about him dressing up in her grannie gown or prancing around in her bras and panties. This does not mean he is a transvestite. He is just hamming it up and letting the fun side of sex out.

• **Initiate.** Many males seem to resent the feeling that it is always up to them to initiate sex. They say they would love it if their partner would, every once in a while, make the first move. What would be so terrible in your saying something like "You wanna fool around?" or "What can I do to make you horny for me?"

After reading this segment on relationships, you should realize that there is more to it than a simple instruction manual, a "do-it-yourself" book that says "face front, raise right hand, grasp him gently." If you feel that you want to do more work on the relationship aspect before moving on, please read the bibliography at the end of this book. Most of the books listed are inexpensive paperbacks, and you would both benefit from reading them.

COMMUNICATION: I CAN'T HEAR WHAT YOU ARE SAYING FOR THE WAY YOU ARE SAYING IT

Most of us are firmly convinced that we are good communicators. We do not have any problems talking, reasonably, rationally and logically. We are also convinced that we are born "good listeners." So therefore, we must be good communicators. Right? Wrong.

We learned by observing our parents, sometimes discussing quietly, but many times yelling, screaming and slamming doors or giving each other "the silent treatment" for days. As children, we also learned little manipulative techniques that got us what we wanted in our family. We threatened to run away, had temper tantrums at the dinner table, slammed doors, or locked ourselves in our room, whining, pouting or crying. We tried them all on for size and found those that worked and used them well. Most of us could easily win an Oscar for theatrics.

Unfortunately, many of us still have not learned how to communicate effectively as adults. Until we are in a crisis situation and start working with a counsellor or therapist, we never look at our interpersonal communications. Then suddenly we realize we have to go back to square one, unlearn all the blocks to communication and learn a whole new way of relating. The very best oral sex is talk.

Empathic Listening and Communicating Skills

Here are some important communication skills for you and your partner:

1. Use "I" terms, statements such as "I feel," or "It makes me feel" or "I am concerned (scared, angry, upset, frustrated)." When you use "I" terms, you are acknowledging that you are admitting to ownership of the problem and not blaming your partner or the world. Instead you are saying, "When this happens, it makes me feel . . . (mad, glad, or sad)."

Let's take a common scenario in many relationships:

Scene 1. Take 1. She is doing the dishes. Her partner pats her affectionately on the tush and her reaction is immediate: "How come the only time you ever touch me is when you want sex?" She is angry, feeling used as a sex object and blaming him. Basically, what she wants to say is "I would really like to spend more time together, just hugging and cuddling and being affectionate, rather than as an overture to sex."

Unfortunately, she turns it around and blames him for not showing love and affection unless he has a hidden agenda. But in the end, he feels rejected, put-down and inadequate, and you can rest assured, he will not touch her again for any reason.

Take 2. He pats her affectionately on the fanny, she leans into the pat, then slowly turns around and looks him in the eye, saying, "Oh, I just love it when you pat me. We used to do it all the time, now it seems as though the only time we touch is as invitation to have sex. Do you miss that loving touch as much as I do?"

With any luck, he will admit that he enjoys close intimate touch, and he would like more. Then he may even risk revealing that he is scared to give her a hug, in case she misinterprets it as a sexual invitation, when all he wants is to cuddle for a while.

The solution is simple. She says "Okay, let's have a distinct signal for sex. If one or the other of us is interested in 'fooling around,' then we can simply nibble on each other's ear, or give a meaningful wink. Otherwise, touching, hugging, holding, brushing, patting, kissing, snuggling and cuddling means just that—fun, touching and body contact." Warm fuzzies.

In this way, you can make your desires clear, without alienating your partner and you have established a behaviour pattern and clear signal system, so you both can get what you want and need, more "non-demand" touching.

2. Avoid attacking, jumping to conclusions and over-reacting. All of these happened in Scene One, Take One. But it could have been worse. She could have accused him of being oversexed, just like his father, and he could have accused her of being frigid, just like her mother. Now that is overkill, hitting a fly with a baseball bat.

Once in a while, you will find yourself flipping back to the old communication habits. When you catch yourself, simply say, "Forget I said that. What I want to say is. . . ." And if your partner backslides and you find yourself reacting negatively, then very gently say,

"I have a lot of trouble accepting what you are saying, because it feels like a put-down to me." The message is clear, you are not into blaming, avoiding or retreating. You are just stating how you are reacting to the old destructive way of communicating.

3. Use appropriate body language. Think about the different moves you make during a serious discussion. You become intense, you lean forward, you watch your partner intently, making gestures that range from pleading to repelling to threatening.

If your partner is trying to explain their feelings to you, and you sit there, stony-faced, arms crossed across your chest, your body language is saying, "You might just as well go bark at the moon. You are not going to convince me of a thing." This is closed body language, and before long, your partner gives up and the subject is dropped, but not forgotten. Rest assured, it will come up again, but the next time with anger and hostility.

This response creates the feeling that this argument is never going to end. So you glance at your watch, wiggle and squirm, gaze out the window, even roll your eyes to heaven. Your partner gets the message, and clicks off. It is over, nothing resolved, nothing solved and a lot of residual bad feelings of resentment, anger, frustration and hopelessness. This means deep trouble, unless you break the pattern of negative communication that is undermining your relationship.

Arguing Constructively

Here are some other hints on how to argue constructively:

1. Practice gentle eye-to-eye contact. Your partner's

eyes will give you a strong sense of how they are feeling.

2. Look at your partner. Observe their hand and head movements. Notice if they are restless or agitated or fearful.

3. Keep your hands away from your face. It may look as though you are trying to hide a grin or a snicker. Never, never shake your finger or point at your partner. This puts you in the role of "critical parent" and they become "rotten kid."

4. Use body motions that encourage your partner to go on speaking. Nod your head and say things like "What happened then?" or "How did that work out?" You can use open-ended statements such as "How did you feel when the counsellor said. . . ."

5. Really listen when your partner is speaking. Do not start developing arguments in your mind to score your point while you are waiting for your partner to take a breath, so that you can jump in, guns blazing and POW, you hit them with your best shot.

6. If there are silences, just let them be. You do not have to rush in and fill up all the spaces with platitudes such as "Don't worry, it will get better soon." Statements like that are quickly rejected and you lose credibility. Silence may mean a natural closure and this is okay. On the other hand, your partner may be gaining insight into the problem or suddenly become aware of a possible solution.

7. It is very helpful if you can paraphrase what your partner is saying, using your own words. That way your partner knows you understand what they are saying.

8. Avoid bringing up touchy topics just before you leave for work, go to a party, go to bed or drive

together in the car. Make a date to talk about it at a more convenient time and place. Or if you are really upset, almost incoherent, postpone the discussion for twenty-four hours. By that time, you may be a little calmer and able to talk about your feelings.

Five-Minute Fight

This is a wonderful strategy that you and your partner can use when you are having difficulty resolving a conflict. Set the timer on the stove or microwave for five minutes. Your partner can use that time to tell you exactly how they are feeling.

You must not interrupt, agree or disagree, show frustration or anger. Listen and try to put yourself in your partner's shoes for that five minutes. Then allow two minutes of silence to internalize what was said. Take the next five minutes to talk about your feelings. This time, your partner must not interrupt or interject. Again, allow two minutes of silence. Then, and only then, can you talk back and forth to each other. Try not to justify yourself, but rather find a compromise solution that will be acceptable to both of you.

It works; try it. You will be amazed how relatively easy it is to resolve some very deep conflicts in a safe, non-threatening atmosphere of understanding and acceptance.

The Other Side of Talking

There is much more to communicating than being verbal and being able to talk about your feelings. The other aspect is listening to hear what your partner is really saying. This is a skill we do not learn in childhood; we learn to hear only what we want to hear. We develop the skill to just click out when our parents are lecturing, giving commands or endless instructions. And we "fake" listening when that seems appropriate. We are "there but not there," making all the token gestures, nodding our head, appearing to concentrate and agree. Then we turn around and do exactly what we want to do, regardless. We've got it down to a fine art.

Then we meet a "significant person," get into a relationship, which is close, intimate, intense. People see us together, totally immersed in each other, absorbing and interpreting every word and gesture, mesmerized and adoring.

Before too long, unless we make a concerted effort to keep in close contact, we both slip back into communication patterns that are not conducive to intimacy. We revert to patterns of pretending to listen, as we did when we were children at home.

If you want to regain that sense of "connectedness" with your partner, you will both have to make a conscious effort to listen to each other. It is more effective if you practise these skills together.

You may well be communicating and listening while you do the dishes or drive down the highway. Many times this feels more relaxed, less stressful and allows time to integrate what you are hearing. But it is impossible to listen while you are reading the newspaper or watching TV. There may be times when it is not appropriate to talk about personal stuff—too many interruptions, no privacy, or there is something special on TV. Make a date to talk about it at another time. Agree on a time and place and be sure you keep the appointment. This shows you are sincere and it is a topic that you feel is important.

If your partner is emotional, or if you find yourself overcome and crying, take a break in the conversation. Then you can say something affirmative such as "This is really upsetting for you, isn't it?" or "I am having a real problem dealing with this. Could we talk about it later on this evening?"

There are some clues that indicate that either you or your partner are not really listening. They include:

• Interrupting and butting in before the speaker is finished.

• Muckracking, digging around and dragging out your partner's past offences.

• Creating distractions, changing the subject, or bringing up other contentious topics as a smoke screen.

• Accusing, blaming or putting your partner on the defensive, making them feel guilty or inadequate.

• Putting together a really "good case" in your head while your partner is speaking. Once they stop talking, you are ready to zap them on that topic. You may feel so confident that you know exactly what your partner is going to say that you feel justified in cutting them off. If this is happening, you are not really listening.

• Running off at the mouth so your partner is overpowered with your verbal diarrhea. Your partner cannot get a word in edgewise, so they simply give up and find another way to get around the problem.

As you read this, you are probably thinking to yourself: "Oh, I don't do that. I am a good listener." But once you and your partner are in therapy, the therapist will no doubt very quickly pick up and make you both aware of your lack of empathic listening skills.

They will then coach you to become good listeners. Once you have mastered that skill, the relationship will improve, and you are almost home free.

Communicating and being heard sounds so simple, but it does not come easily. We have to practise till it becomes second nature—and the only way to relate to those we love.

Filtering Does Not Help

Many times, you may be reluctant to discuss a problem because you feel that it may upset your partner and they will not be able to handle it. In that case, you are treating your partner like a child. You are saying, "I do not think you are ready for this. I know what is best for you and I am going to protect you." Presumably, your partner is an adult, capable of dealing with most issues in life and you are shielding them from reality.

Now, that does not mean that you should come on like gangbusters and dump a whole load at once. And it is important to look at what you are telling your partner and why you feel it is necessary to tell them right now. Think about whether you have a hidden agenda—perhaps to gain power and control?

You may also be tempted to filter out information or feelings that you think could threaten the relationship or that might be used against you in a future argument. In a loving, trusting relationship, this would not be necessary. An example of this method of "covering your butt" occurs in the following letter:

Dear Sue,
The other night I was coming home from an office party and I was sexually assaulted in the

*underground parking. Sue, I just cannot tell my part-
ner. He would say I must have been asking for it, that
I had been flirting at the party, and that it was all my
fault. It wasn't, but I just cannot go through the has-
sle of trying to convince him. Now he says I'm acting
strange and he thinks I was fooling around with another guy. Should I tell him about it?*

Think of the anguish this poor lady is going through.
The assault is traumatic enough, and she does not
have the love and support of her partner to help her,
only the fear that he will reject her. I hope she will go
to a rape crisis centre for counselling and that her
partner will be involved at a later date. That would be
the time to start looking at the lines of communication in that relationship with an eye to developing an
open honest way of relating to each other and to increase the trust level.

Don't Analyse to Death

When you and your partner first start to use your
new communication skills, there may be a tendency to
analyse every word and every move. Then you lose
much of the spontaneity and are afraid to say or do
anything for fear it will be misinterpreted, so that
you're always walking on eggs. You dread hearing the
words "I feel," and so much of your time together
seems to be spent navel gazing that the joy and fun are
gone.

There are some good books that can help you with
communication skills—some old, some new, but all
relevant. Please check the bibliography at the back of
this book.

TOUCH: CREATIVE CUDDLING

We place a great deal of importance on what we say and how we say it. But our body language says as much as the words we speak. Standing in front of your partner, fists clenched, feet firmly planted, jaw thrust forward, is more appropriate to the command "Take the damn garbage out" than to the loving statement "I love you so much."

Watch a couple who are in love and observe how their bodies communicate. They lean towards each other or they lean on each other. They are in constant, close, physical contact. He touches her hand; she tucks in his collar. They are hand in hand and arm in arm, touching every chance they get. Their eyes never leave each other. They watch each other like hawks, and they gaze long, loving looks into each other's eyes. The intensity is palpable; it is electric. We watch them and kind of smile, remembering the days when we were like that.

We wonder, what happened? We still love each other, but somewhere along the way, we feel we lost it. Not really, there are times when it comes back in flashes of intimacy and closeness. But on a day-to-day basis, we assume that we "know" our partner; we can anticipate reactions and responses, so, we do not have to watch every move they make and interpret how it applies to us. Then, every once in a while, they surprise us and we have to sit up and take notice once again, or we gain a new insight and become reawakened to our partner.

If there is little or no physical touching throughout the day, then you will notice a gradual pulling away.

Remember when you passed each other in a doorway, the way you would lean forward and physically brush each other? You had that sense of connectedness and an awareness: "Wow, it is still there for her, too." To avoid that body-to-body contact you would have had to suck in your gut. Now, if you pass in the doorway, you try to slip by without touching your partner; they would probably do the same thing, and before you know it, you are both avoiding each other.

Then, you become aware of the absence of physical contact and gradually you begin to realize, "The only time we touch each other is when one or the other of us is interested in sex." This becomes more exaggerated till you are saying to each other, "The only time you touch me is when you want sex."

From there, things disintegrate rather rapidly. He avoids all touch, afraid that it will be misinterpreted, and she, feeling used, thinks "I'll be damned if I am going to touch him. He'll just wanna get into the sack." So all intimate contact is totally avoided and your sex lives deteriorate dramatically.

On the other hand, your body language can also give the message that you are "approachable," that you are open, receptive, appreciative and that you would love a nice warm fuzzy type of hug. We have all heard the statement: "Four hugs a day for survival, eight to grow and twelve to flourish and blossom." Sounds like a great prescription.

Everyone Needs Touching

Research clearly shows that babies who are cuddled, hugged, rocked, nuzzled, sung to and cooed are more content, happier, not as fussy, and they like lots of people. Babies who are deprived of this tactile stimulation do not thrive as well. Research has also shown that male babies are touched differently than female babies. For male babies, it tends to be "rough house" type of touch. Baby boys are held up in the air and gently shaken rather than snuggled. Little boys are more often left to "cry it out and get over it," while female babies are picked up, comforted and attended to. The need for loving body contact does not stop once they are toddlers, but all too often this need is unmet.

By the time they reach adolescence, the amount of loving touch has decreased for both males and females, but more dramatically for males. Teenage females will no longer sit on daddy's lap. Daddy has subtly indicated that "now you are a woman, this is no longer acceptable." She, aware of his discomfort, pulls away and refrains from great, long, warm "fuzzy" hugs. But she can and does still hug mother, aunts, grandparents. And she has no hesitation about hugging her girlfriends, holding hands with them, walking down the street arms around each other. A male on the other hand, will shake hands with his grandfather, give grannie a quick peck on the cheek. His mother may ruffle hair, that's it. He seldom touches dad, and never brothers or sisters. Touch deprivation leads to skin hunger.

Then comes adolescence with non-stop sexual feelings, what we call the time of the "galloping gonads." He gets turned on over nothing—the slightest "skin to skin" contact with almost anybody and he is horny. But it is not acceptable to be horny amongst other males. This implies that you are "homo" (homosexual). So the only contact with other males might be a pat on the ass, if you score the winning points in the basketball game, or to rub your helmet enthusiastically, if you score a touchdown in the school championship football game. If you are always randy around females, then you are a "pervert." Actually, you are perfectly normal, but nobody ever told you that. So, a male, denied touching and loving affectionate contact, equates touch with sex and sexual feelings. Then if an attractive female teen touches him, holds his hand, he immediately equates it with SEX. He then has this "humungous" erection, and he wants to die of embarrassment, all because they touched. And if she touches him again, it is interpreted as a definite "yes" to sex.

This explains so much of the misinterpreted, unspoken messages that contribute to date rape. She touched him, and he is convinced that it is permission to "go for it." Even if she said, "No, stop—" he may be firmly convinced of the old myth that once a male is turned on, he must have sexual release or he will explode or die of terminal "blue balls." He feels that it is her fault; she was asking for it. Wrong. But nobody told him that all he has to do is go home and masturbate. This is normal and he will feel better.

Males are never encouraged to simply say, "I need a hug," That might indicate neediness, weakness and dependence on other people. In order to maintain their aura of success and self-sufficiency, most males are reluctant to be seen as weak and vulnerable. So guys "self censor" and deny themselves the body contact that we all need and crave. Females may ask for a hug from other females or a male who is felt to be safe, but will hesitate if there might be sexual implications.

I am convinced that before you start on any therapy for relationship or sexual concerns, it would be beneficial for you to go back to "square one" and learn to touch each other, to "non-demand touch." Sit together on the sofa holding hands or arms around her shoulders, massage his neck, just touching, close, intimate but with no hidden agenda such as "sex later."

When you are ready, take the plunge. "How would you like a back rub?" No "wink wink, nudge nudge," just a warm, loving back rub. And no expectations that as soon as you have given the back rub, your partner will automatically reciprocate. Another time yes, but this is not "tit for tat." You can feel that wonderful sense of love and intimacy coming back—all without sexual connotations. Once you get this far, you are over the hump, and getting there is half the fun.

By now, you realize that the biggest sex organ of your body is your skin. Now move on to enjoy all the sexual arousal feelings, but this time it's different. The expectation that you will have sexual release is put on the back burner. For now, the focus is on making comfortable contact with your own body and your partner's body.

CHAPTER 3

STUMBLING BLOCKS TO SEX

● ● ●

MYTHS ABOUT SEX: THAT'S A CROCK

Sex is the one area of our lives that is dominated by myths or misconceptions. Some of them originated with religious belief and have persisted and become incorporated into our sexual convictions. Many of them stem from the false premise that males have a natural superiority over women.

Earlier civilizations worshipped women as goddesses or as earth mothers, such as Gaial. In the Jewish, Christian and Muslim faiths, people worship one God and he is male. In these religions, men are vested with more power and are elevated above women. Many people still hope their first-born child will be male.

These attitudes affect the relationships between

47

men and women, and create problems in their sex lives. In particular, women have felt "controlled" in their sexuality and in their sexual pleasure. An example of this is the preference for the "missionary position" (male on top) during intercourse, a position that reinforces male superiority and female passivity.

There are also myths relating to females—people believed that women who were menstruating contaminated the kitchen and caused milk to sour. Even today some religions consider women "untouchable" during menstruation. Another form of control on female sexuality is in teaching our female children that they are not to be sexual in any way till they are married. Of course, the idea is that women should keep their virginity until marriage. Though you may not believe in these taboos, they still have an effect on how women feel about themselves. Making women feel inferior ensures that they don't enjoy sex—apparently, if they did, they would run rampant, leading to the ruination of males and all of society!

Some of these controls are loosening to a degree, and you can see how our concepts of "sexual morality" have gradually been modified as they pass through succeeding generations. Yet residual overtones continue to influence us. Many parents still hope their daughters will remain virgins until the honeymoon. We have a double standard with our sons. There is an unspoken message: "Boys gotta sow their wild oats." We shrug our shoulders and hope they do not get a disease.

Gradually, some of our myths are giving way to new information and facts. The only way this happens is through education and information. Let's look at a

few commonly held myths and misconceptions:
- Sex is dirty. (Save it for the one you love.)
- The only thing guys are after is sex.
- Women use sex to get love; men use love to get sex.
- Females are most interested in sex during ovulation.
- If a woman says "no," she really means "Coax me a little."
- A frustrated man soon develops "blue balls"; women do not suffer if they don't reach climax.
- Only gay males and druggies get AIDS, never women.
- If a male ejaculates, that always means he has reached orgasm.
- "Bigger is better"; women prefer a man with a big penis.

This last myth tells males that it is essential to have a big penis to sexually satisfy a female. Wrong. When the male with the smallest, non-erect penis has a full erection, it will be only a few millimetres smaller than the man with the large penis and full erection. Not only that; the top two-thirds of the vagina has few nerve endings, while the bottom one-third of the vagina is loaded with wall-to-wall nerve endings. The male with the smallest erect penis will penetrate the bottom one-third of her vagina, and that is where the action is. What is the point of having a huge nine-inch penis banging around up near the top of the vagina when there is nobody home up there. Waste of talent, guys. Relax. It is what you do with what you have that matters.

Breast size is another big myth. Large-breasted

women are supposed to be more highly sexed than their "flatsie" sisters. Wrong. There are as many nerve endings in the breasts of a well-endowed woman as there are in those who have terminal flats. But just think, there is a lot less area to cover for the small-breasted woman to get the same stimulation. So Ms 28A is just as sexy as Ms 44D. Relax and enjoy your body just as it is.

The myths about orgasm abound. Females expect the earth to move the first time they have intercourse. Reality is it seldom happens the first time. In fact, women will not likely reach orgasm until they are relaxed and comfortable with their partner, the trust level is up, and they are experienced enough to just let it happen. But some women never get there. That does not mean that they cannot enjoy their sexual activity. It can be pleasurable, satisfying, intimate and still good sex.

Another commonly held myth that we need to dispel is that when males have sex, they generally have an erection and usually ejaculate. This feels good and is pleasurable, but it does not rank a ten on the Richter scale. Then, every once in a while, he is super-aroused and ejaculates with spectacular gusto and pleasure. For him, that is orgasm, and nobody expects that to happen every single time. Females do not look their partners in the eye and say "Didja cum? Better luck next time, big boy." (It is not that we don't give a damn, but we do not feel we are to blame if he does not come.)

It is also a misconception that a male can get turned on in a flash and has what we call the "ever-ready penis" which springs into action whether or not he wants it to. If that is not bad enough, it is thought that females have an "ever-receptive vagina"—that women can lie there, anytime, anyplace, and just let it happen.

Reality is there are times in any woman's life when sex is the last thing on her mind. Women may not be into sexual gymnastics but have difficulty being honest about it and so resort to: "Not tonight, dear, I've got a headache," or "I think I hear the baby crying."

While we are on the topic of orgasm, what about the recent myth that sex is best if you both climax together? Totally wrong. When either the male or female is at a high level of sexual arousal, they are totally focused on the pleasurable sensations they are experiencing right now. They are aware their partner is there and involved, but they are really into their own sensations when approaching orgasm. For the other person, much of the pleasure comes from watching the partner's enjoyment, seeing them respond and feeling very competent as a lover. Now, if you are both into simultaneous, spontaneous, multiple orgasms every time you have sex, you will be wondering what is happening for your partner: "Should I slow down, or maybe I had better speed up?" you are not focusing on yourself; instead you are trying to read your partner's readiness. No fun at all.

As we grow up, we are all convinced that "Our parents don't do it." We believe that sex is the prerogative of the young. Once you reach forty, forget it; you are too old. Now as we grow older, we keep advancing the age, but we still have the idea that sex is for the young and the beautiful and any day now we will stop it. As young people are better educated about sex, I hope they will examine these ideas and attitudes so that they can be more accepting of the older folks around them, including their aging parents.

As I go through the different segments of this book, I will include the correct information for some of the most common myths and misconceptions. Be sure to read the section "You Are What You Are Because of What You Were When." Share, compare and update what you learn with your partner and friends. It will be much easier to fully enjoy your own sexuality and give pleasure to your partner.

FEARS OF SEX, UNRECOGNIZED AND UNSPOKEN

It is quite understandable how easy it is to have fears about sex. Since earliest childhood, your parents likely controlled your sexual behaviour by instilling fear. Unless you had good sex education and information, these fears persist and affect your sexual performance and pleasure.

Let's list a few fears:

• Fear that you are not normal, you are oversexed, a pervert, a homosexual or a danger to society.

• Fear that sex will be painful. A young female wrote:

Dear Sue,
Does it hurt the first time you have sex? Do you bleed
a lot if you are a virgin?

• Males sometimes fear that they will hurt their partner during sex. One young guy wrote:

Dear Sue,
My penis gets so big when I masturbate. I am terrified that I will tear a female if we have sex. Is this possible?

• Fear you will turn your partner off, if you have "vaginal farts" (during the thrusting of intercourse, air trapped in the vagina that "flubs" out after withdrawal of the penis).

• Fear of unplanned pregnancy.

• Fear of diseases, including chlamydia (a sexually transmitted disease) or AIDS.

• Fear from total ignorance and misinformation. A young male wrote:

Dear Sue,
I am a seventeen-year-old male and I am terrified that if I have sexual intercourse, my penis will get stuck in her vagina. I have watched dogs screwing, and sometimes the male dog cannot pull out. Does that ever happen to people?

• Fear of not doing it right, being laughed at, being rejected or having friends find out you are a sexual dud. Not all fears are groundless, but facts and information can put them into a better perspective.

Fear of AIDS

One of the latest fears is what I call "AFRAIDS," a fear of AIDS that is not based on fact but on misinformation. Some people are still convinced that they can get AIDS from kissing or from a toilet seat.

According to the latest evidence, the human

immunodeficient virus or HIV virus that causes AIDS is spread four ways only: (1) by sexual contact with an infected partner involving the transmission of body fluids; (2) by sharing needles in doing drugs; (3) through blood transfusions; and (4) by prenatal transmission from a mother to her unborn child. The virus has also been detected in tears, saliva, urine and feces, but the small amounts involved make it unlikely that transmission is effected through these means.

Very simply, unsafe sexual contact means having sex without using a condom properly every time you "do it." It is possible to get AIDS from oral-genital sex if one partner is infected. Please read the section on "Oral-Genital Sex" for more information (see pages 114-123).

Sharing a dirty needle when "shooting up" heavy-duty intravenous drugs is also high risk behaviour.

The third way of spreading the virus is through a blood transfusion from an infected donor. In Canada and the United States, there is an intensive screening process and all blood donations are tested before being used for a transfusion.

Most people know this information, but have difficulty communicating their concerns to a potential partner. It really takes courage and experience for someone to say to their partner: "I don't know much about AIDS, but I do know that I am scared, and I am sure that you are, too. I would enjoy sex much more, and I am sure you would, if we did not have to worry about this or any other disease." Then continue to talk about it: "I was wondering if you have ever had unprotected sex with somebody who could be infected? Have you ever done heavy-duty drugs? Have you ever been involved in anal sex without protection—without a condom?"

Once you have gotten through this discussion, move on to talk about using condoms and practising safer sex. Then you must make sure that the condom is used properly every time you have sex.

This process takes courage and a positive self-image. But practising safer sex is an essential survival skill today.

The realistic fear of AIDS makes the need for fidelity in a relationship more crucial today as well. It has also increased the determination shared by couples to make their relationship work. Hence, a book like this, which emphasizes communication, intimacy and trust, should be a valuable asset for couples who are committed to a monogamous relationship. Learning problem-solving skills and techniques will make your sexual partnership more pleasurable than having outside flings. By being able to work through sexual problems and dysfunctions, you can get sex back on track once again.

STEREOTYPES: SHOULDS AND OUGHTS

Until recently, both males and females had very different and distinct roles. For a woman, the expectation was that you would find a man, get married, settle down, have babies and live happily ever after. Males were the breadwinners, the providers for the family. They helped out in emergencies, but they were not any more involved in parenting than was necessary and usually didn't enjoy it.

Women were supposed to be intuitive, nurturing, tender, emotional, tending to resort to tears to get what they wanted. They were expected to be moody, unpredictable, weak and inclined to gossip. In terms of sex, women did not take the initiative and responded to romance—candle light and wine, a box of chocolates, a dozen roses and soft music. "Sweet nothings" like, "I love you, I need you, and I want you," "you are the greatest" and "I will never leave you" whispered in her ear were expected to put her "in the mood for love."

Men, on the other hand, were supposed to be strong, brave, fearless, aggressive, adventurous, independent, emotionally stable, leaders and achievers with highly analytical brains. When it came to sex, they were expected to make the first move and never take "no" for answer. They got turned on by nudity or by even thinking about sex. And if they got horny, watch out. Men were considered the animals and it was women's responsibility to keep them under control or satisfy them.

This role stereotyping, or moulding of people to meet the needs of family and society, did make life easier for people who could accept those expectations and constraints. You knew what was expected of you and you just did it, no questions asked.

But you were locked into these stereotypes and, if you did not fit into the mold, males were classed as "wimps" and females labelled "cheap and easy." Once you got a reputation, it was very difficult to lose it, short of going into the priesthood or becoming a nun.

Recently, people have begun to question whether these stereotypes are really valid, finding that they couldn't express their own individuality and uniqueness because it wasn't "lady-like" or broke rules like

"Real men don't eat quiche." For example, today many women continue their careers after they have children, and many men are sharing more of the parenting. Suddenly men are realizing how much their fathers had missed by excluding themselves from active parenting.

Gradually, we are beginning to accept our androgyny—learning to enjoy the masculine aspects of being female and the female components of being male. This new awareness was initiated by feminism, and the "trickle effect" is that males are also liberating themselves from the constraints of their stereotypical roles. But we still have a long way to go in shedding the old stereotypes. There are many males and females, who like things the way they were in the good old days, when men were men and women loved it.

Even today's "liberated" youth cling to some old stereotypes. I was doing a presentation to about 1,700 "frosh" students at a major university. I was teaching safer sex (stressing "no condom, no sex"), and I talked about the fact that some smart ladies are carrying condoms in their purse for a heavy date.

The guys in the audience went crazy. There were such comments as, "She is a slut, a sleaze-bag, cheap, easy, the local bicycle, everybody has a ride." Old ideas die hard. I am not sure I was able to convince them that she was one smart lady. She knew the risks and was not willing to take a chance. But she was also not going to allow the absence of a condom to stand in her way. . . .

I hope we all continue to question our old attitudes and values about the stereotypical male and female and the roles we are supposed to play.

CHILD ABUSE AND OTHER BAD NEWS

> *Dear Sue,*
> *Four months ago, I met a really wonderful man. He is kind and patient and I really like him. He likes lots of sex and in the beginning we had sex at least once or twice a day and it was great. But now he is lucky if I can bear to be touched once a week. He thinks it is his fault and that he doesn't turn me on anymore. What he does not know is that I was sexually abused by my step-father when I was twelve. I seemed to be able to put it behind me and was coping okay until now. Now I do not want anybody to touch me at all and certainly not sexually. I am scared I am going to lose him.*

As this letter shows, sexual abuse, which includes incest (any form of sexual touching by any member of the family) or sexual assault (any forced sexual activity without the person's consent), can interfere with sexual responses and pleasure later.

Only recently have we become aware of how common sexual abuse is. It is estimated that one in four women are the victims of sexual abuse—either assault or incest. It is also estimated that for every five females who are victims, there are two males who have been sexually abused. Males are reluctant to talk about sexual abuse and few report it, which means that the frequency of male abuse may be higher than the statistics indicate.

In any case, we are dealing with a problem of major proportions for both males and females. Unfortunately, there are not enough good, qualified, experienced and affordable therapists and therapy groups available. But getting therapy for the trauma of incest and sexual assault is essential for sexual survival. This is not something you can resolve by yourself. You may be able to bury it for a while and appear to cope, but it does affect you. As the above letter shows, sexual abuse can interfere with your sex life any time, even when you think things are going well.

Children Are Vulnerable

Incest generally begins when children are quite young. Children are powerless because they are smaller, weaker, less knowledgeable, and dependent on adults whom they have been taught to respect and obey. Because children are curious, because they want to please adults, because they simply cannot understand why anybody would want to harm them, and because they do not have the skills to say "stop that," they are not able to get out of threatening situations. This is why they are vulnerable to incest or sexual abuse.

Many children are reluctant to report incest, fearing repercussions in their family. After all, they were probably told: "If you tell anybody about our little secret, Daddy might have to go away. And you wouldn't want that would you?" They are also hesitant about disclosing the secret for fear that the abuse might shift to a younger brother or sister.

Some children may tell a parent or relative, but often nobody believes them, or they are sent to a child psychiatrist. And because the kids are scared, they change their story. Or the professional may not believe them and they are sent back into the family to be reprimanded as a trouble-maker.

Incest brings about personality changes, but it is difficult to confirm the diagnosis based on changed behaviour. Some of the most obvious changes are: school work is affected and marks drop; eating habits change; sleeping patterns change. A child may become restless, fearful, cry at bedtime, have nightmares, become withdrawn and refuse to be involved in family activities. A child may also withdraw from friends and may not trust any adult and become suspicious of all males.

Children who are victims of incest or sexual assault may also become sexually precocious, displaying knowledge of sexual behaviour. They may be flirtatious and behave in a way that is not appropriate for their age. They may use sex appeal to get what they want. After all, it was sex and silence that got them that new bicycle from Daddy or Uncle George, and maybe they can use sex to con cousin Henry into buying them a new stereo. It's the way the abusing adults have taught them to respond.

If nobody picks up on these clues and stops the incest, the child may run away and become a "street kid" or may develop short-term "coping skills" that allow them to survive, but not live fully.

Effects of Child Abuse in Adulthood

Many victims of incest will have difficulty establishing a relationship with a partner in adulthood. They are unable to trust, to communicate, to establish intimacy, and they avoid all sex. Others appear to be able to put the negative experiences behind them, to fall in love and enjoy great sex for an indefinite period of time. Then suddenly a particular smell, a specific touch, a sexual move may trigger a sudden flashback. All the old feelings of revulsion, of anger, of powerlessness may flood back in an emotional storm.

Partners, not understanding what preceded this outburst, blame themselves—"What did I do wrong?" —and feel rejected.

Males who are victims of incest or sexual assault (rape) suffer the same emotions. Generally, they are less willing to seek therapy, believing that as a male, they should be able to cope with their feelings of anger and resentment. They tend to believe that once they fall in love it will all be better. But they often find it difficult to establish an intimate relationship with a partner until they manage to get some help.

Incest also affects all areas of a person's life. It is estimated that between 40 and 70 percent of women who were incest victims have a chemical dependency on drugs or alcohol.

We do know that kids who disclose and receive help, support and comfort from other members of the family and are able to get some counselling change from being victims to being "survivors" who are able to be intimate and sexual in a loving relationship.

For those of you who have gone through these negative sexual experiences in your past, I would strongly urge you to get help through individual therapy, and later, when you feel ready, progress to group therapy which is very effective. You may even, in individual therapy, remember incidents that you have forgotten but which are still affecting you.

Once you have gained some insight into the effects of sexual abuse on your self-image and on your ability to relate in a close, loving, intimate relationship, then sex therapy for different dysfunctions will be much more effective.

There is a wonderful book called *Secret Survivors* by E. Sue Blume. It is "must" reading for women who are victims of incest. Please see the bibliography on page 223 for more books to help you.

CHAPTER 4

MORE TROUBLE

• • •

SEX IS BORING

Remember that mad passionate "can't-get-enough-of-each-other" feeling that you had in the beginning of your relationship? You had non-stop sex all weekend long, and now, you find yourself thinking, "Do I really want to have sex tonight?" You scare the hell out of yourself when your answer comes back: "No, not really —but I think I should." If you are honest with yourself, you will probably find that you could now describe your sex life as ranging from "ho-hum" or a yawn to monotonous, repetitious or predictable. We call it "ennui," the sexual blahs. The spark is gone. If sex happens, it is usually on a Friday night, after the late night news under the covers with the lights out.

Whatever happened to the frenzied fervor of past sexual romps? Now the moves seem scripted and uninspired, and you know exactly where his hand is going to go next and exactly what it is going to do. "Yup, there it goes." Hot and heavy has now settled into b-o-r-i-n-g.

You are realistic enough to know that not every meal is going to be a gourmet delight. Every once in a while, you get to eat leftovers. So it is with sex. But every once in a while, you also want to get out of the sexual doldrums and that sexy nightie isn't enough anymore. So now what?

I cannot give you specific suggestions that are guaranteed to work for you. You have to think SEX and be innovative. There are a few ideas scattered through this chapter, but the ones that will be the most successful will come from you.

Think of your sexual fantasies. Ever wondered what it would be like to have sex in a sleeping bag? For forty dollars you can get a cheap sleeping bag and wrestle in there. If you break the zipper, no problem. Spread it out in front of the fireplace or on the beach. Try the balcony and give the neighbors something to talk about. If it doesn't work, use the sleeping bag as a dog bed.

Don't stop there. Rent an erotic video (available from most convenience stores). Set the scene with candles and incense. If you can't do it with the person you love and trust, who are you going to do it with?

Use your imagination. Dress up as a bag lady, then slowly strip down to some very skimpy lingerie. Or you could take a few strips of soft cotton cord and tie him up, spread-eagled, and then pleasure him with a feather until he begs for release. Total cost, zip; and fun worth a fortune.

So far, I have focused on females being innovative, but males can do it too. Guys, remember "your song," the theme song that could trigger all those warm mushy feelings when you were together. Even now, when you hear a certain "golden oldie," you get mellow and sentimental. Why not make a tape cassette of all your favourite love songs—yours, not necessarily hers—because this is your gift of your special memories. That should do something.

How about writing a love letter or holding her hand at a romantic movie? A few years ago, there was a hit movie simply called "10" featuring Bo Derek, and the passionate sexual sequences had Ravel's "Bolero" as the musical theme. Even now, anybody who saw that movie and now hears that musical beat immediately has a flashback to those steamy scenes. Simple. Besides watching the movie, you could go to the library, borrow "Bolero," and play it at an appropriate time. Wanna bet it works?

The expression "if you don't use it, you lose it" applies to your imagination as well as to your genitals.

PREMENSTRUAL SYNDROME

Dear Sue,
Premenstrual syndrome (PMS) is the bane of my existence. I have a wonderful life, a great husband and family. But about ten days before my period is due, I become "instant bitch." I rant, rave and roar, hate

myself and everybody else. I am aware I am doing it, but am unable to stop, or if I force myself to stop, I get depressed. It sure affects my sex life. My poor husband is "punch drunk" from my verbal battering which lasts until my period comes. What can I do?

PMS is also called premenstrual tension syndrome. There are over two hundred different signs and symptoms of PMS ranging from headaches, feeling bloated, general malaise, panic attacks and phobias, tender breasts and migraines.

The results can be devastating as everybody runs to hide from your raging moods. And the moods may cause upheaval in your relationship with your partner. Afterwards, you may feel guilty and may overcompensate the rest of the month.

Do see your friendly family physician for confirmation of your diagnosis. If you are on the birth control pill, your doctor may take you off. If you are not on the pill, you may be put on the pill for a few cycles to see if that helps. Some doctors prescribe a ten-day course of oral progesterone, starting three days after ovulation.

And there are a few things you can do for yourself. It is a process of elimination to find what helps. Here are some suggestions:

• Take a short course in stress management. Try to reduce the pressure and anxiety of "overload" in your life. PMS seems to affect "supermoms" more commonly than others.

• Try increasing the vitamin B intake in your diet. Higher intake of B6, B12, folic acid and niacinamide is also recommended, along with 300 units of vitamin E daily.

• Eliminate all caffeine from your diet: tea, coffee, cola, chocolate. Also reduce your salt intake dramatically. Some doctors insist you eliminate alcohol entirely.

• Get into a daily exercise program, establish a regular sleep pattern, and grab a cat-nap whenever possible.

• Quit smoking now! This is difficult, but think of the benefits. And your family will realize you are serious in your determination to eliminate your PMS.

• Discuss PMS with your family, so they understand what is happening and can be supportive and helpful.

Once your PMS is under control, and you feel better about yourself there will probably be a dramatic improvement in your sexual relationship, too.

It is sure worth a try: what have you got to lose?

WE ARE TOO OLD FOR THAT KIND OF STUFF

Dear Sue,
I am a happily married 51-year-old female, and I am having real difficulty coping with this menopause bit. The worst part is sex is impossible. My vagina is dry and cracked and sore, I get a lot of yeast and bladder infections, and sex is the pits. Will this last forever?

The answer is no, but let's take a look at what is happening.

After puberty, probably one of the most dramatic life cycle changes to affect self-image, sexual desire and performance will be "the change" or "the change of life."

In women, we refer to it as menopause, the natural end of menstruation and ovulation, and the gradual reduction of monthly hormone cycles. Because the ovaries, which secrete estrogen, stop working, the amount of estrogen drops and the body tries to adjust to the absence of these hormones. This generally occurs between the ages of forty-five and sixty.

Males do not menstruate, nor do they ovulate, but they do experience what we call the male climacteric, the reduction of male hormones. Both males and females may experience many of the same symptoms of the climacteric. They both develop facial wrinkles, including "turkey neck" and "crow's feet" around the eyes, "age spots" or "liver spots" on the skin, along with stretch marks and cellulite. Women may experience a thickening of the waist and sagging of the breasts. In males the chest may sag to become a "Molson muscle" around his waist. Both males and females feel less urgency about sex, take longer to become sexually aroused and have a reduced need for ejaculation or orgasm. The good part is that both men and women take more pleasure in touching, hugging, cuddling, and snuggling.

There are some differences between males and females. Males suffer more anxiety about sexual performance and are more inclined to feel inadequate because they are afraid of sexual failure.

Most females during menopause experience "hot flashes." The gradual cessation of menstruation and ovulation leave many of them feeling less feminine, attractive, appealing or interesting. Other physical changes in women include decreased vaginal secretions. The vaginal walls become thinner and more vulnerable to irritation, and tears or painful cracks occur which reduce sexual pleasure and may even lead to dyspareunia (painful intercourse).

Studies show that one-third of women have few, if any, symptoms of menopause; another one-third have noticeable but tolerable side effects; and another one-third experience distress and seek medical advice. Most of these women respond well to HRT or hormone replacement therapy. During that week, there may be a slight "withdrawal bleed" almost like menstruation.

Before you family doctor will prescribe HRT, you will need a complete physical exam, including a pelvic examination, a breast examination, probably a mammogram (special type of X-ray of your breasts).

There are some things that menopausal women can do for themselves. Some women benefit from vitamin supplements, including the vitamin B complex, vitamin C and some women are convinced that vitamin E is helpful too. Following a regular exercise program also helps, as does keeping up your outside interests and activities. Be sure to get plenty of rest and eat a well-balanced diet.

Now, it ain't all bad; there are some real blessings and benefits to "the change." No more worries about pregnancy or contraception; no more periods or PMS. Males are no longer blessed with embarrassing spontaneous erections, premature ejaculation or sexual frustration if they do not ejaculate. Sex can be calm, comforting, warm, and reassuring, with a lot of touching, cuddling and snuggling, and that sense of togetherness, without the pressures for performance and passion.

You are still sexual and, once you are aware of the changes in your body, you can modify your expectations of what sex will be like as you grow older. This letter pretty well says it all:

Dear Sue,
I am an eighty-one-year-old male who still likes sex. It has changed; it now takes all night to do what I used to do all night. But it is so much better—just that sense of joy in sharing the warmth of body contact and close intimacy. I feel sorry for older people who are alone. They are missing so much.

A study from Sweden has found that elderly people who are sexually active stay vital and more physically active. They are more alert and have less memory loss than those who are celibate.

You are sexual from the day you are born till the day you die. Enjoy all of it.

There is a wonderful book called *Love and Sex After Forty: A Guide for Men and Women in Their Mid and Later Years* by Robert Butler and Myra Lew. Check it out.

PARTNERS HELPING OR SCUPPERING THERAPY (FOR SEXUAL DYSFUNCTION)

I must admit, I do have problems with the terminology "sexual dysfunction." It sounds so ominous, so terminal, like the kiss of death. I really prefer to think in terms of a concern. And when a concern becomes severe enough, it prevents satisfactory function. By satisfactory, I mean satisfactory for either one or both partners in the relationship. There may also be a valid sexual concern or anxiety, when a person is not in a relationship, which is even more intimidating. "If it won't work right when I am all by myself, how is it ever going to work with another person?" This thought of sexual incompetence can be so overwhelming that a person will not even attempt to establish a relationship with somebody.

In a relationship, dysfunctions are almost always tied in with relationship problems; so for successful therapy these must be addressed. If there is anger, resentment, distrust, dislike, these feelings will begin to manifest themselves in sexual activity. Intense dependencies or feeling powerless and feeling out of control over what happens in your life can often lead to hostile feelings. Most people cannot openly express their feelings of hostility, without the overriding conviction that the relationship will break up. So the anger and resentment finds an out through a sexual dysfunction.

This is why it is essential that you read this whole book, cover to cover before you focus in on any one specific "problem area." This is also the main reason why you will progress much farther and much faster if you have a therapist who can keep you on track and help you along the way. Therapists with broad experience recognize and can help you work through your fears of being rejected. Rejection takes many forms, from "Not tonight, dear. I've got a headache," to the tacit understanding "You go to bed early and get up early, and I will go to bed late and get up late. And that way we can avoid each other without having to confront the issue of *sex*."

Unfortunately, many, many couples are reluctant to

seek counselling when their relationship starts getting into trouble. They know something is wrong—that conflicts are not being resolved and that anger and resentment are compounding faster than the interest on their mortgage. But they are reluctant to confront it and work towards resolving the issues. Without good communication skills, the problems get worse as they blame each other, argue and fight. Unfortunately, by the time many couples do become involved in therapy, it may already be too late. So much damage has been done that it is beyond resurrection. The one thing that I would recommend is that as soon as you feel that things are getting out of control, as soon as you do not like what is going on, make time to talk about it and get moving towards finding some help.

Destructive Games Couples Play

Denying sex to punish your partner is a way of getting even: "You would not let me go out with the boys, so I'll be damned if you are gonna get sex (closeness, intimacy, satisfaction or pleasure) from me."

This is clearly a power struggle. He is saying, "The only way I have any control is in sex. You dictate every other aspect of our lives. You can't have it all your own way." So he withholds sex, psychs himself out of an erection or prevents ejaculation, just to show her who is calling the shots.

Another neat ploy is sexual sabotage. You are angry with your partner, so you find the one area of his sexual function where you know he is vulnerable and you subtly reinforce that inadequacy. Remember the old joke, "Question: What are the four most damaging words in the English language? Answer: Is it in yet?"

That will do it every time. We sometimes play on each other's fears of sexual inadequacies or failure. Games like this drive a huge wedge between partners and may affect sexual performance in the future.

"Muckraking" is another neat game. Wait for the crucial point in an argument, then start a knock-down-drag-out-hoot-and-holler fight to distract from the issue you are discussing. Your partner becomes confused, unwilling to continue the fight. So you win by default.

Delaying tactics work. "I'll just check the baby (finish watching the hockey game, unload the dishwasher, balance the checkbook)." By the time you get back, your partner is asleep. Then you play the next scenario of that game. Wait until they are asleep; then nudge them and ask, "You still awake?" When you don't get a reply you pull a "righteous indignation act" the next morning: "How come you didn't wait up for me?"

A subtle way of avoiding sex is to repulse your partner by not smelling very good, having dirty greasy hands, bad breath, or burping or farting in bed. You might also go to the extreme of gaining so much weight you are not interesting or attractive.

Being uncooperative is another tactic. She likes receiving oral sex, so he develops an aversion to even touching her genitals. Or he wakes up with an erection and wants to cuddle, and she rolls over and goes back to sleep.

Another game occurs when one partner starts playing "Red Cross nurse" by expressing officious concern for the other partner. This letter presents a clear picture of this situation:

Dear Sue,
Sometimes when my wife and I have sex, I lose my
erection. Now, I know this happens every once in a
while to all males. But my wife claims she is not satis-
fied unless we have intercourse and I ejaculate. She
says she isn't interested in sex until I get cured. But I
think she has the problem, not me. Am I right?

Her message is "I'm really okay, but I will be even better as soon as we solve your problem." She is shifting
the focus from her own role in the problem.

A therapist will recognize these "sexual games" and
can help find out why they are being played out. A
good therapist can also help find another way to get
the messages across—the right messages rather than
twisted, destructive versions.

Even in therapy, one partner may take a lofty stance,
offering to help the other partner find the cause of
the problem. From this position, they will analyse and
offer suggestions that only serve to make the partner
feel totally inadequate. The therapist must recognize
the behaviour, then help both partners identify what is
happening and redirect them to prevent this game
from continuing.

Many couples find it beneficial to write out the reasons they have sex, then rank order them and discuss
their priorities. It may help identify the games they are
playing. Besides passion, they may have sex to release
anxiety and tension, to have a baby, as proof of their
identity as male and female, to escape loneliness or
grief, as a demonstration of power, or to express a full
range of feelings from love and tenderness to anger
and destruction. We may feel that this is flawed, but we

must realize that in every loving relationship there are some feelings of aggression and the desire to gain power and control.

If a couple carries on these negative games, they are working against their relationship and their therapy. They cannot expect to gain much from talking with a therapist, calmly, coolly and rationally. When at home, they lash out with the anger that should have come out during the therapy session. This is counter-productive.

Some people go to therapy just so they can say they had marriage counselling. Their heart is not in it, and they have no intention of allowing it to be successful. Basically they want out of the relationship. This "tokenism" is dishonest and unfair to the partner who may be committed to making a go of it.

WHEN AND WHERE TO GET HELP

If Your Partner Refuses

There are numerous reasons why people are reluctant to seek counselling for relationship or sexual problems and wait too long:

• What if my friends found out? They would think I was crazy.

• I don't trust a stranger. I don't talk about my problems to strangers.

• It costs too much; I can't afford it.

• I don't know where or how to find a therapist.

• It takes too long; I haven't got the time to spare.

• All therapists are crazy. They need help more than I do.

• I tried it once and it did not work.

• I am scared I will have to face stuff that I am not willing to deal with right now.

• It is too late or I can't change (can't means won't try).

If you have suggested counselling, you may well find your partner rejecting the idea outright or at least being less than enthusiastic. The partner may try to reassure you that all is just fine or indicate that you are making something out of nothing, "it is all in your head." But, if you are feeling threatened or uncomfortable in your relationship, then you have to realize that you need help, and you are not going to get it from your partner, so you must get the help yourself. Make an appointment with a therapist and go by yourself. You can talk about your feelings, your reactions, your fears, knowing that this will definitely be beneficial in helping you cope with your feelings. You can focus in on the problems in the relationship, understand how they affect you and the way you react, thus helping you find a more effective way of responding. Talking about it with a counsellor will give you some insight into your partner's problems too. You may simply discover how to accept your partner as they are, or, how to effect change.

When you go to a therapist, be realistic; you may decide that you do not want to stay in this relationship. If this is the case, counselling will help you clarify that you want out and make the move easier without evoking bad feelings between you and your partner. Work towards resolving the problems and feeling good about yourself and your feelings. Try to gain some insight into the cause of the break-up, your role in the break-up and what you can do to prevent it from happening again.

If the relationship appears to be generally healthy, but you or your partner are experiencing some sexual problems, please realize that they will not go away all on their own. Go for help—fast.

If you start therapy alone, there may be subtle changes in your attitude and behaviour that intrigue your partner and they may want to find out what this is all about. Or your partner may feel that this therapist is getting a lopsided picture of the problem without input from the other side. Your partner may want to see the therapist in "self defense." Many times, the therapist will see your partner alone first to get some sense of his or her role in this relationship. This also gives the therapist an opportunity to reassure your partner that the therapist is not prejudiced or taking sides and to provide reassurance that this is not going to be a "win-or-lose" battle of the sexes. Then the therapist will bring you both together for a counselling session.

If your partner does not want to be involved in counselling, but the therapist feels that both of you are necessary for a successful outcome, then the therapist may contact your partner. The therapist may say something like "Betty Lou seems to be having a problem with one aspect of your relationship, and I feel that you could really help her out. Would you be willing to come in to meet me and we can discuss it?" Most partners would respond positively to that invitation.

If your partner still refuses, go alone. You can still benefit from the counselling, gain some coping skills for yourself, and have a forum in which to decide whether this relationship is worth your effort.

Reasons for Wanting Counselling

Besides a sexual dysfunction, there are other reasons for seeking professional help: depression, feelings of hopelessness or despair, suicidal feelings; conflicts with either set of relatives or your own or your partner's children; physical illness, pain, menopause or male climacteric; fears of homosexuality or lesbianism for yourself or for your partner.

Perhaps alcohol or drug problems are affecting your relationship and sexual activity. Sexual assault or sexual abuse, either in the present or in the past, would also be valid reasons for seeking therapy.

We must include day-to-day problems that affect our self concept/self-esteem and relationships: job, money, in-laws, recreation, religion. Children sometimes compound the problems—whether to have them and what to do once you have them.

Where To Get Help

Once you have decided to seek help, where do you find a therapist? Well, if you have a family doctor, ask for a referral. If finances are a problem, in Ontario the only therapist covered by medical insurance would be a psychiatrist or a family physician who does in-depth counselling. Most family physicians don't. It is too time consuming and many doctors do not feel qualified to do therapy.

The average session costs between seventy-five and one hundred and twenty-five dollars a "therapeutic hour" (fifty minutes counselling time). This may seem expensive, but think of it as an investment in your future and the survival of your relationship. Then it is a good investment for the buck.

Other good sources for finding a therapist are your friends who know of somebody, or somebody in your family who may have had a great counsellor in the past. Ask your family doctor for the names of a few therapists. No luck? Well, look in the Yellow Pages under "Marriage and Family Counsellors" and select one who has a credible degree in social work, a medical degree, or a degree in theology, or psychology. It is likely the certification as "marriage and family counsellor" ensures that these professionals have some training. If they belong to an association of family therapists and counsellors, they should be suitable. Perhaps your place of employment has counselling services which could give you a referral. Public health nurses generally know of some good therapists, or your minister, priest or rabbi may have special training or know someone who is a skilled counsellor.

In most provinces, there are family services organizations who do counselling for a very reasonable sliding-fee scale. Once you have found somebody you are comfortable with, it will take a few weeks to get your first appointment. In the meantime, there are a few things you can do to give yourself a head start in terms of insight and openness to change. Check the list at the end of this book for other books listed under specific topics and areas of interest or concern to you and your partner. New books can be found in any bookstore under the headings of "Health" and "Psychology." Pop psychology books can often be very helpful, if you and your partner read them and share your reactions.

Try keeping a journal and write out your feelings as they come to you. Do not worry about the writing, spelling, grammar, punctuation. Just scribble. It is for you alone. Make it very clear to your partner and family that nobody else is to read your journal and if they do, they will have to deal with their own reactions. You do not need to explain, justify or apologize for what you have written. Journals are very therapeutic. They help you focus and clarify. Once you have written out your feelings, you might be able to put some things out of your mind and not worry them to death.

"Self-talk" is another practice that is helpful for many people. When you are all by yourself on a walk or alone in your car, stuck in traffic, or when you are exercising or jogging, verbalize your thoughts and feelings aloud. Thinking aloud can help you clarify your thoughts and feelings and "sound them out." Sometimes it can be a rehearsal of what you would like to say and how to say it without alienating your partner. This works very well.

Friends can be invaluable if they are not into giving advice or "rescuing you," but are willing to listen, to just accept what you are saying and be there for you.

What to Look for in a Therapist

Of prime importance is finding a therapist you trust, who you know will not reject you, put you down or laugh at you or your actions. Confidentiality must be guaranteed, and information you give must never be revealed to your partner or family. Your therapist should be supportive and non-judgemental.

Good therapists never give advice such as: "I think

you should" or "If I were you, I would." Instead, they will outline all the alternatives available to you, help you anticipate the eventual outcome of each alternative, and then encourage you to decide which would be best for you. They should not push you to explore areas that you are not ready to get into right now.

They will ask you to verbalize your feelings and conclusions, and will allow you to experience all your feelings of sadness, anger and joy. A good therapist will never talk down to you or pat you on the head and say, "There, there, it will be all better by tomorrow." You do not need that panacea.

Occasionally, you will feel that you are "stuck," that you are not making any progress. Then suddenly you may make a breakthrough and you're on a roll. Other times there will be a sense of quiet resolution. It is all wrapped up, you have dealt with it and there is a sense of closure, of completion.

Therapists do not solve your problems for you, but they will help you gain the ability and skills to solve your own problems. Then you do not have to run to a therapist every time you have a problem; you can solve it yourself. You can prevent problems in the future by recognizing the warning signs, then cut them off at the pass.

It helps if you and your therapist, very early on, have outlined the basic problem; then the underlying problems. What event actually tipped the scales and got you to accept the need for counselling? What are your long- and short-term goals? When you have an objective, you and the therapist agree on an unwritten contract: things you will do and things that your therapist will contribute.

Since most sexual dysfunctions are basically relationship problems, you need to be prepared to work on your relationship. Some therapists assign homework: strategies that you do for yourself. Sometimes your partner will do similar exercises and then you share and compare. You will both benefit if you do your homework, be that "paper work" or touching practices or massage. Never taught you that in school. . .

Dear Sue,
I recently watched a TV show, "L.A. Law" where one of the main characters fainted whenever he saw a naked woman. So the therapist, to "desensitize" him, disrobed seductively. Does this happen in real life therapy? If so, I am going to find myself a gorgeous male therapist.

Therapists are professionals and, as such, any form of sexual relationship with their clients or patients is absolutely taboo. The client is needy, vulnerable and easily exploited. If the therapist betrays the client's trust through sexual overtures, it is regarded as abuse and the therapist can legally be charged.

About ten years ago, some sex therapists were utilizing the services of surrogate sex partners who were trained, skilled substitutes to help the client overcome their sexual dysfunction by being involved in sexual activity with them. The client was then supposed to take their newly gained skills back and share the information and techniques with their partner.

It was a great theory, but all too often the client would form an attachment to the surrogate. The patient would feel that the surrogate understood them so well and knew exactly what to do to help; their ego was stroked by a person who was attractive, knowledgeable and innovative. The client transferred their affections to the surrogate and the original partner became jealous, threatened and resentful. The therapy might have been successful, but the primary relationship was usually doomed.

Today, surrogate sex partners are not used by qualified sex therapists in Canada; they are legal but seldom used in the United States.

If you are in therapy, the minute you feel even slightly uncomfortable—if there is a "meaningful look" or any close body contact—leave immediately and cancel all future appointments. If the therapist checks up on you, simply say you do not wish to continue therapy and stick to your decision. Then find another therapist immediately and report the incident. You will need to talk about your responses to the incident.

You may find your therapist is unwilling to pursue one particular area of concern. For example, one man wrote:

Dear Sue,
I am currently seeing a psychologist because I avoid intimate relationships with women. I know I am not homosexual and I desperately want to love somebody for life. I was molested when I was a little boy, and whenever I bring it up, my therapist promptly changes the topic. Should I stay with my therapist or look for another one?

If you feel a topic is worth pursuing, but your therapist is avoiding it, you have two choices:

1. You can tell your therapist that you really want to work on that area of concern. Be assertive and insistent. You could even tell the therapist that you feel they are avoiding that one particular problem.

2. You can tell the therapist that you feel it is crucial to solve this problem so you can move ahead in therapy and that you are unhappy with their lack of response. Then you can locate another therapist who will deal with this issue.

If you make the first choice, it may take a few weeks before you are certain that you will be able to continue working with this therapist. If you still don't feel you are making any progress, find another therapist.

I am firmly convinced that all couples would benefit from some relationship counselling after they have been living together for six months. Catch the little problems before they become big ones.

CHAPTER 5

WHAT TO AND HOW TO . . .

● ● ●

There are elements common to most sexual activity that can either heighten pleasure or stand in its way—depending on how you interpret and respond to them.

FANTASY

Fantasy may be defined as sexual activity confined to the mind.

Dear Sue,
Every time I am alone on a bus or in the library and I
see an attractive girl, I immediately flip into a sexual
fantasy. In my fantasy, she is young, inexperienced

but curious and willing. We do wild and crazy sexual things together. Fantastic. But reality sets in, she looks at me, I smile, and she moves away. Does she know what I am thinking?

Everybody fantasizes—in a line-up at the grocery store, while stuck in traffic on an expressway, over a pile of ironing or during a very boring meeting. It can be a pleasant daydream or sometimes it can be a sex fantasy. No problem. Sex fantasies are an escape, a wish fulfillment, heightening of sexual pleasure. They are safe, harmless and enjoyable.

Everybody has their own personal, favourite sexual fantasies—images of what you might like to do, what you find exciting. You probably have a dozen or more in storage, and when the time is right, you review them and haul out your "personal best." Sometimes you develop a new and different fantasy to add to your collection.

Female Fantasies

Males and females appear to develop slightly different fantasies. Research shows that women seem to prefer less physical action-packed fantasies; rather, they focus in on romance, tenderness, love, being "carried away in the heat of passion over which they have no control." A young woman wrote:

Dear Sue,
Just before I go to sleep at night, I let myself fantasize about being with some guy. He slowly unbuttons my blouse, kissing me passionately and telling me that I am irresistible. Slowly his hand moves down . . . Sue, I get wet just thinking about it.

Harlequin Romance novels, afternoon soap operas and tender love songs are all designed to feed into female sexual fantasies.

Most women do not emphasize any "rough stuff"—pain, force, violence or brutality. They may fantasize that some male finds them so sexually appealing that he becomes instantly aroused, so unable to control his animal passion that he cannot stop and she dissolves into his loving arms, surrendering to his burning desire. But in a female fantasy he would never drag her into the bushes and force her to perform oral sex.

The most common female fantasy is sexual intercourse with a loved partner. The next most common fantasy is to be slowly and seductively undressed by a male who knows exactly how a woman likes to be touched. Females also list oral sex, either performed by them or being performed on them in a passionate but gentle, loving manner.

Male Fantasies

Male fantasies are more physical, with themselves doing the action. Their fantasies are more explicit, focusing on the sexual areas of their partner's body, like the size, shape, colour and erectness of her nipples; the colour, curl and texture of her pubic hair. Her genitals are fantasized as enlarged, engorged, throbbing or pulsating, dusky-coloured and wet.

Dear Sue,
When I lie on the beach, I watch a beautiful female spreading sun-tan lotion on herself. Then I fantasize putting lotion on her body myself. I undo her bikini and spread lotion over her breasts, and her nipples

become erect, and it really turns me on. I have to roll over so nobody sees the bulge in my bathing suit.

Males also fantasize about their partner having an earth-shattering orgasm, moaning and gasping, clawing and clutching, in a frenzy of passion. Males fantasize sex in an orgy with multiple partners and performing non-stop. Many females share this fantasy. If it is agreeable to both partners, they may search and find like-minded people for a *ménage à trois* or a foursome for "swinging."

Guilt and Fears of Fantasies

Research shows that both males and females who have good sex education and are sexually experienced have more frequent, vivid, explicit sexual fantasies than people who have strict moral values or repressed sex experience and limited sex education. People who are inhibited about their sexuality also have a much higher level of guilt and will consciously tend to repress fantasies because they are seen as abnormal.

Sex is composed of fantasy and friction. Most people fantasize during sexual activity; it increases the level of arousal and reduces familiarity, repetition and boredom. Many times, this fantasy involves people other than their partner. This can lead to a great deal of guilt and fear, because they interpret it as infidelity. After all, one of the ten commandments is: "Thou shall not covet thy neighbour's wife, nor his ox nor his ass nor anything that is his." And then there's the biblical quotation, "If any man looks at a woman with lust in his heart, he has already committed adultery."

Religious injunctions aside, if you check your fantasy, you will likely find that the fantasy partner's image is vague, blurred, unfamiliar; the face is unclear, not anybody you recognize. This fantasy does not pose any threat to your love or sexual relationship; it is common, safe and harmless. Don't waste your time feeling guilty.

Frightening Fantasies

Fantasizing is a private act that you can control and direct to your own comfort level. Some fantasies may scare you, if you see them as abnormal or dangerous. The following letter is an example:

Dear Sue,
I am an 18 year old male and sometimes I scare myself because I have this fantasy of me having sex with my best male friend. Does this mean that deep down I am more attracted to him than I am to my girl friend? I hope not. . . .

However, this is not an unusual fantasy. You also need not worry that you are a "latent" homosexual if you have some "same sex" fantasies. This is completely normal. Everybody has them and they do not serve as an indicator of homosexual tendencies. If they are your predominant fantasies—if they are your most pleasurable and produce the highest level of sexual arousal—they may indicate that your sexual orientation leans towards homosexuality. But there would have to be many more indicators, so take lots of time before you become convinced that you are gay or lesbian. It is not something you have to decide by midnight tonight.

The occasional sexual fantasy involving force or violence, incest, sex with children, kinky sex involving beastiality, or exhibitionism might be cause for concern. These kinds of fantasies indicate that you might do well to seek therapy.

> Dear Sue,
> I have fantasies about being dominated by a female. I fantasize verbal humiliation, spankings and whipping when I masturbate, and it really turns me on. But I worry about it. I don't know how I got this way and I wish I could stop. I would like to get married and have kids, but I am afraid I won't be able to grow out of this fantasy.

Obviously, this male is upset by his fantasy and he is feeling that he has no control over it. But it is essential that you know that a fantasy is just that—a fantasy, a daydream. Fantasies are not reality; you do not have to act on them. You have the power to decide whether you want to make your fantasy into a reality.

If you want to stop a particular fantasy, you can use a form of aversion therapy on yourself, called "thought stopping." Every time you find yourself into a fantasy that makes you uncomfortable, pinch yourself hard enough to cause pain. Then force yourself to think of something else. Gradually, that one fantasy will be equated with pain, and you will soon put it out of your mind.

If your fantasy of choice becomes increasingly violent or "abnormal" and includes force, coercion, exploitation, or involves people who are powerless—and if the urge to act out your fantasies is becoming stronger—then please get professional counselling immediately. This is very important.

Sharing Fantasies

Most people do not share their fantasies with anybody, not even their most intimate friends or lovers. But sharing sexual fantasies with your partner can certainly spice up a boring sex life. First you have to decide how much you are willing to share, and have a pretty good idea just how far your partner might be willing to go with your fantasy.

Nancy Friday, in her book *My Secret Garden*, says that smart women know how much of their fantasies their partner will want to share. She also states that you will not have achieved complete trust and intimacy, until you have been able to share fantasies with your partner. I have some reservations about this point of view. I am sure that you can have a truly intimate relationship without "telling it all." If you think that it might have a detrimental effect on your relationship, if you feel uncomfortable, or if it would put pressure on your partner to fulfil your fantasy (love in a canoe), then I feel that "discretion is the better part of valour." You can still enjoy it as a fantasy, but don't rock the boat of your relationship.

If you wonder about other people's fantasies, if you feel that yours are really abnormal or kinky, or if you want to increase your fantasy stockpile, you and your partner might enjoy Nancy Friday's book. It will likely make you feel as though you are totally unimaginative—dull and boring, but very normal!

There is a great book on men's sexual fantasies, too.

It is called *Men in Love,* and it's also by Nancy Friday.

EROTICA AND PORN

Say the word "pornography" and people frequently become very upset. It is a very controversial issue for most women and many couples.

Many people including most females are repulsed by pornography because the stories, pictures or videos generally depict females involved in sexual activity against their will. They may be shown tied up, or being whipped, or in exaggerated positions (spread-eagled over the hood of a car, for example). The variations are endless; some are more violent than others, but the woman and occasionally the men—are depicted as getting off on the torture. Not most women's idea of a fun time.

Erotica, on the other hand, is sexually explicit litera-ture, art or music that is not degrading to males or females. It does not depict violence, force, coercion, manipulation, exploitation or pain. It generally is in a loving, caring, tender context, showing romance, woo-ing or courtship. Most people enjoy erotica and find it quite acceptable and sexually stimulating for both partners.

I have a collection of letters from women whose partners use porn for sexual arousal. One woman wrote:

Dear Sue,
My boyfriend will often read Playboy *or watch a porno video, then roll over to my side of the bed and*

*want to make love just like he saw in the video. I feel
he is having sex with me but making love to the blond
bimbo he was watching on the tape. It just turns me
right off.*

Let's examine the range of feelings that this woman
may be experiencing:

• She may feel inadequate, comparing her own
body to "the body beautiful" centre-fold which does
not have a wrinkle, a blemish or a bruise, with no cellulite and no stretch marks. Ninety percent of women
would not qualify for Miss July, but they still are fully
sexual human beings.

• She may also feel threatened, fearful that he is
going to leave her for somebody who does enjoy sex in
"unusual" situations.

• She may be frustrated, trying to keep up to his
sexual idiosyncracies.

• She may be terrified that he is going to get into
really kinky sex that might be dangerous.

• She may feel like a sex object, used and manipulated.

The extensive use of porn may result in a real rift
between the couple unless they are able to talk about
it; how he feels about it, why he enjoys it, how it affects
his feelings about his partner. Her reactions and responses must also be heard and understood and accepted as valid.

If she threatens to break up with him, he may
promise to abandon the practice. But deep inside he
may resent it and feel he is being deprived of a pastime he sees as harmless and pleasurable. He may
promise to give it up but still keep his collection of

magazines or videos hidden away. If his partner ever finds them, then there has been a real break in the trust level. She may feel deceived and disappointed and may have trouble trusting him again.

Some males may take a "like it or lump it" attitude; then the partner will have to decide whether she can continue in the relationship. She may decide to tolerate it, but the resentment may remain just below the surface. This relationship problem may require some counselling by a therapist to find a solution that is acceptable to both.

On the other hand, some males may also find that pornography has a negative effect on their self-concept and self-esteem. The males in the pictures always have enormous penises, and erections that go on forever. Not many males can live up to these unreal expectations.

Women have their own kind of erotica, even pornography. Women's porn is generally "soft-core porn," usually romantic. "He tenderly stroked her secret places where no man had ever touched before." The most popular women's erotica is probably Harlequin Romances, and now, in response to popular demand, a new series has come out called "Harlequin Temptation," which is a little more racy and sexually explicit.

Erotica, even some soft-core pornography, can be beneficial in adding some spice to a sex life that has become boring, dull and monotonous. Some couples read it aloud to each other. Many couples watch erotic videos together, becoming sexually aroused, then they make up their own ending.

Some women do enjoy hard-core porn, but most

regard it as degrading to women and do not enjoy the violent, forceful or brutal activity. Statistics show that *Playgirl* magazine showing nude males is very seldom purchased by women, but generally by homosexual males.

Many women whose partners use porn extensively fear that the behavior will escalate till it becomes a compulsion. They may be concerned that he will need that kind of violence for thrills and will eventually sexually assault her or some other woman.

So we see that erotica and some pornography may have a positive effect on a sexual relationship, or it can be very detrimental. If you find you are unable to resolve the conflict, it might be a good idea to make an appointment with a counsellor.

MASTURBATION

When you are young, it seems as though "masturbation is the occupation of the nation." Teenage males have so many slang expressions for masturbation, from "hand job" to "jerking off" or "beating your meat." I must admit, I cannot recall one that is used by females except "playing with yourself."

Masturbation is defined as either solitary or mutual touching of the genitals and other erogenous (sexual) areas for sexual stimulation, pleasure or release. It has a long history. Drawings depicting masturbation appear on prehistoric cave walls and are common in Greek art.

Formalized religion, such as Christianity, Judaism, and Islam, all declare masturbation a sin. In the Bible, the "Sin of Onanism" is from an Old Testament story of a man whose brother had died. It was customary for the surviving brother to immediately have sex with the grieving widow and impregnate her so the family line would continue. But Onan refused to do this. Instead he "spilled his seed upon the ground"—many people believe this refers to masturbation. In fact, his "sin" was in disobeying the religious law by not impregnating his sister-in-law. But over the centuries, it has been interpreted as the sin of masturbation. This has been reinforced by the Catholic Church's emphasis on sex for procreation, rather than for pleasure.

Even those who are not religious are sometimes convinced that this form of "self-abuse" is a perversion and a health hazard, causing insanity, shrinkage of the genitals, acne, warts and congenital abnormalities for future children.

Parents in Victorian times tied their children's hands down at night, or applied a "penile ring" with protruding metal spikes which would poke into the penis if they had an erection in their sleep. Females had a type of "chastity belt" clamped on to prevent them from touching their genitals at night.

Interestingly, Kellogg's Corn Flakes and Graham Crackers (named after Sylvester Graham) were developed when people were convinced that a high-fibre diet would eliminate masturbation.

We now know that masturbation is perfectly harmless; it is a normal and natural release of sexual tension. There is a wonderful "one-liner" that goes "Ninety-nine percent of all males masturbate regularly and the other one percent are liars."

Now, I would never accept these as valid statistics

because there are still many people, brought up in some families and certain religions and cultures, who have been taught from earliest childhood that masturbation is morally wrong. They may have tried it once, and they felt so guilty, so embarrassed, and so ashamed that it was not a pleasurable experience. For them, this is normal and natural, and we must not make them feel abnormal or that they are missing out on something great.

But most young males do masturbate, some more frequently than others. This should not be considered a problem, as long as it is not done compulsively, to the exclusion of "hanging out" with their friends, being involved in sports, hobbies and social activities.

If it becomes an over-riding pastime, if a person comes home from school, retreats to his room, stays there till bedtime with barely time out for dinner, then we would be concerned, but not about the masturbation. We would worry about this person's withdrawal from everyday activities. Masturbation would merely be a symptom of his withdrawal from living. This person would need counselling to help him cope again, to develop social skills and an improved self-image.

Fears of Masturbation

Teenage guys going to school hear horror stories of bad things that will happen if they masturbate. Though they may not stop masturbating, many believe these tales and worry about the following things:

• You will go blind, bald, grow hair on the palms of your hands or get severe acne—all announcements to the world of what you have been doing to yourself.

• Your brain will turn to mush, so when you fail a

math exam, masturbation gets the blame, not the fact that you were masturbating instead of studying.

• You will hurt your penis, wear it out or, if you continue to masturbate, it will fall off. I have heard of guys who measure their penis before and after masturbation, just to be sure.

• You will reduce your sperm count, so that, when you want to have a baby, you will be "shooting blanks."

• You will become "addicted" or "hooked" on your hand and not interested in sex with a partner.

• You will become homosexual—only "gays" masturbate. Most males have some "same sex" fantasies and are concerned that they might be homosexual, and this just "confirms" their worst fears.

All these fears and anxieties are groundless and our teenage males need good extensive sex education to help them accept themselves as normal, sexual human beings. Even if, as an adult, you know these are myths, they can go on causing fear, guilt or shame.

Females Do It, Too

Contrary to popular opinion, females can and do masturbate. The injunctions against it are very strong. At a very early age little girls get the message, loud and clear: "Don't touch yourself down there. You will hurt yourself; you will get an infection. Nice girls don't do that. You will ruin yourself, lose your virginity and no man will want to marry you when you grow up." More than males, females buy into these parental and societal injunctions (young males tend to persevere surreptitiously in spite of parental warnings and threats). It is not unusual to find teenage females who have never taken a good look at their own genitals, identified

their clitoris and their vagina and located their urethra. Doing this would mean that they would have to
take a mirror and a bright light, put one foot up on a
chair or lie down, flop their knees open, separate their
labia majora and *labia minora* and really look. Too many
teenage females regard this as "gross."

There are some females who are not ashamed to
admit that they started masturbating at a very early
age. They explored and touched their genitals, al-
lowed themselves to become sexually aroused, and
learned how to bring themselves to orgasm. They
soon realized that nothing bad happened, and it sure
felt good. One sixteen-year-old female wrote:

> *Dear Sue,*
> *When I sit on the floor and watch TV, I have one heel*
> *under my tush and I move back and forth. It feels*
> *wonderful, is that masturbation? Wow, it feels great.*

We now know that these women, as they mature, will
have far fewer sexual inhibitions with their partners,
and are most likely the ones who thoroughly enjoy
sex, and are easily orgasmic.

The most successful sex therapy happens when we
are able to teach women how to masturbate, how to
pleasure themselves, without guilt and shame. These
women will then know what sexual "moves" work for
them and can guide their partner to incorporate this
into their foreplay and lovemaking.

This section, combined with the section on
"Fantasy," are probably the most important segments
of this book for women to read and practise.

Males should read these sections too, because most

males have no idea that females "do it," least of all the female they are sexually involved with. At first, many males are threatened to learn that she can "do it" herself without any help. Once males accept that their partner can and does masturbate—and it does not mean he is not sexually satisfying her or that she is a nymphomaniac—he may realize that her ability to satisfy herself means he does not have to worry about keeping her sexually happy, then the performance pressure is off him and sex can once again become spontaneous and fun.

Many people, both males and females, are convinced that women always use a vibrator to masturbate. A vibrator or a "dildo" is an imitation of a penis. Some males feel anger and resentment that they can be replaced with this plastic device and are afraid that she will get to like it more than she likes the "real thing." Fact is, they don't need to be afraid of being displaced by a battery-operated, mechanical tool.

Very few women reach orgasm through intercourse, but rather through clitoral stimulation. So, she may use the vibrator for clitoral stimulation, or she may insert the vibrator into her vagina and mimic thrusting. It is only for arousal, and seldom will she reach orgasm this way. She will probably stroke the clitoris to bring herself to a climax.

Perhaps she will teach you how she likes the vibrator to be used for stimulation, and if, for some reason, you do not want to have sex, you can bring her to orgasm with the vibrator.

Some couples use a vibrator during intercourse. She holds it up against her clitoris during intercourse for increased stimulation, or she may hold it against the base of his penis or around the scrotum during intercourse to increase his arousal. And, shocking as it may seem to many of you, some males find they become very sexually aroused when a vibrator is gently massaged over their penis, testicles and around the rectum. So, imagine all the fun you can have for an investment of $4.98 or so (batteries not included).

So now you know: masturbation is normal and natural and harmless for both sexes, and it does not stop just because you are having sex on a regular basis. Masturbation is never in competition with sex with your partner; it is in conjunction with sex with your partner. If you accidentally discover your lover masturbating, relax and don't think you have to jump in there and prove that the real thing is better.

We also need to be aware that, with our aging population and the number of "older sexual seniors" who do not have a partner or who do not or cannot have intercourse, masturbation is still the one pleasurable sexual outlet easily available. We need to give all people permission, even encourage our seniors to enjoy their sexuality, either with a partner or alone.

There is a significant finding that Masters and Johnson proved in their research. The level of sexual arousal is higher with solitary masturbation than it is with sexual intercourse or mutual masturbation. When you are becoming sexually aroused, you focus completely on the sensations, the pleasure and your body responses. You are able to do this fully if you do not have a partner to think about. (Where are they at? Are they just about ready "to come"? Should I hurry up or slow down? Are they getting bored, enjoying it, or turning off?) All you have to think about is yourself and enjoy. And you are totally free to do exactly what will please you, exactly when you want it done. You do not have to guide or direct your partner. You can just do it with great abandon. This applies to both males and females.

The disadvantage is that there is no intimacy, no sense of "connectedness" or closeness, no sharing the joy of participating in your partners responses and pleasure. And there is no touching, holding and hugging. You may feel very alone, untouched and unloved, but physically satisfied.

One way couples overcome this is to masturbate themselves, but together, cuddling and kissing beforehand and afterward snuggling together.

There's More than One Way to . . .

One of the most common questions I get is: "Sue, how *do* females masturbate?" While males are innovative in their masturbatory techniques, they cannot imagine how women can possibly do it. Many *women* cannot imagine how women do it. Here are a few of the techniques used by some women. Please remember that there is no right or wrong way. Through the process of elimination, you decide which ones work best for you.

Some women squeeze their legs and thighs together in a rhythmic movement varying the pressure on their clitoris. A few lie hanging over the edge of a bed or couch, rocking and squeezing their legs together to provide gentle friction to the clitoris.

Sliding down a banister adds a sense of speed and excitement. Many women straddle the arm of a chair or chesterfield, or they pad the rim of the bathtub with a big towel, straddling it and rocking back and forth. Some get off on climbing trees, riding horseback or riding a bicycle, especially one of those racing bikes with a long skinny seat.

Dear Sue,
When I was a young girl, I discovered that running water over my genitals felt good. I still do it, even if I'm not sure it's appropriate for a grown woman, and sometimes I think I should stop.

I wonder where she got the idea that it was not appropriate for a grown woman. It is normal and healthy and quite okay.

Many innovative women have a removable shower head so they are able to spray a stream of water over their genitals—you know, "Don't turn on the shower, let the shower turn you on." You could lie down in the bathtub, slide towards the faucet, put your legs up on the wall and allow warm water to flow over your genitals. If you are lucky enough to have a jacuzzi, lean up against the spigot and allow the water to swish around your genitals.

Rather than a plastic vibrator, many women use a zucchini, a large fat carrot, a cucumber, a candle—no end of ideas.

Most women simply touch, stroke or rub their genitals with their fingers. And there are a few who become aroused, even experience orgasm while they are doing aerobics, sit-ups or push-ups. "Whatever turns you on."

Women have an extensive repertoire of masturbatory practices from which to choose. They appear to be more innovative than most males who seem to rely on the "five palm sisters" for masturbating. No matter what you do, masturbation is usually accompanied by a great sexual fantasy.

Unfortunately, many people, mostly women, say "I can't do it." If they absolutely refuse to look at their attitudes and values in the light of new information about the safety and normality of auto-eroticism, then there is nothing more we can do to help them. Unfortunately, they will be settling for less than the very best. We can only hope that in the future they will give themselves permission to enjoy solitary masturbation.

A How-To for Females

You may have experimented with masturbation, but because of your feelings of guilt you may not have really let yourself go with it. You may have had difficulty allowing yourself to get into a sexual fantasy that was sexually arousing for you. So, here we go: Do-it-yourself masturbation for women.

Your first homework assignment is to use a small hand mirror and take your time, relax, and take a look at your genitals. Separate the *labia majora* and *labia minora* and locate your clitoris, which is a small round organ barely protruding from under the folds of the labia. This organ is equivalent to a man's penis. It is super sensitive because it is loaded with nerve endings—as many nerve endings as a male has in his whole penis.

Very gently touch your clitoris, either by stroking it or in a slow circular motion. You will notice these movements give a pleasurable sensation and that your clitoris will respond by becoming erect, exactly as a man's penis does when the head or gland is stroked. You will also notice that, if you are too rough or the movements are too fast and jerky, the clitoris will become over-sensitive and irritated and it will not be pleasurable. Be gentle.

Still using your mirror, shift your focus down to a small indentation below the clitoris, above the vagina. This is the urethra, the tube through which your urine travels when you urinate. It is a very small opening and sometimes difficult to locate.

Below the urethra you will find a much larger opening, oblong, not symmetrical, pink and fleshy. This is the *vaginal orifice* or opening. Now, if you have never had sexual intercourse, have never participated in heavy-duty petting, never used tampons, then the hymen, that thin mucous membrane that partially covers the vagina, may still be intact. If this is the case, you will not harm yourself in any way if you very gently insert one finger into the vagina and examine the interior walls. Feel how soft and "cushy" they are, how the walls stretch or expand if you press outward, and it does not hurt. Repeat this exercise until the hymen is relaxed and stretched sufficiently to admit three fingers without discomfort. Continue touching till you locate the areas that are very sensitive to touch and stimulation. Experiment. Find out which type of touch feels best, what direction, and how much pressure.

By now you will notice that the area is very moist with a clear mucous liquid called "lubrication." This is your body indicating that you are getting ready for sexual activity and intercourse. You will continue to lubricate until you are very sexually aroused and then less lubrication will be produced. This lubrication makes intercourse easier and more pleasurable.

Insert your three fingers a little farther up into the vaginal vault. Feel the rounded "dome," called the *fornix.* You will also be able to identify your *cervix,* a round organ protruding into the top of the vagina that has a small opening in the centre, just like one nostril. This is the *cervical os* leading to the cervical canal and on up into the uterus. Be aware of the sensations. When you push upward on your cervix, you can feel your uterus move in your abdomen. Amazing.

After you have become comfortable with the sensations, and have even found them enjoyable, withdraw your fingers and sniff them. Yes, you read it right. Smell your fresh vaginal secretions. See, they do not "smell bad." Granted, they have a very distinctive, unique odour. They say that this odour is the true aphrodisiac for males. We should bottle and sell it, better than "Joy" by Patou!

Now that you are familiar with your genitals and have accepted them as you (and even like them); now that you have learned which areas respond to touch and what type of touch triggers pleasurable sensations—do exactly what you think would feel good for you.

You may find it a little difficult if you come from the old school that says: "This is wrong" or "This is a waste of time." You know better. So now accept that, relax and enjoy. Do not make it a chore. It is a delight.

Develop the ambience that you like—low lights, perhaps candle light and soft music. Take a long leisurely bubble bath, touch yourself, your breasts, your nipples, your legs, your thighs, your abdomen.

When you are towelling yourself, admire yourself in a full-length mirror. Appreciate yourself. You may never make the centre-fold of *Playboy* but that is not important. Acceptance, approval and appreciation are what matter here.

Please be sure that you have read the section on "Fantasy," because your next homework project for yourself is to call up one of your old reliable sexual fantasies and do for yourself exactly what you think would feel good at that particular moment.

You may be curious about using a dildo or vibrator. As they are inexpensive, why don't you invest in one and experiment. Here is a wonderful letter from a mature lady:

Dear Sue,

I had reservations about buying a vibrator. What if I died and my family discovered it when going through my things? They would think I was abnormal. One day my kids and I were joking about it, and I mentioned my curiosity and they were gung-ho for me to try it. I did and I really enjoy it. Why did I need permission from my children to do what I wanted to do?

Many women incorporate a vibrator into their solitary sexual activity, as well as into their sex play with their partner. "Try it. You may like it." You may find that you have one orgasm, and are still turned on so you continue to stimulate yourself and have a few more. Some women say they "come" in waves, one after the other, as long as the stimulation continues. Other women "take a break," then re-stimulate themselves all over again. Don't worry that you will become addicted to the vibrator or to "do-it-yourself" sex.

Once you have brought yourself to orgasm, you will feel like a kid who has a new toy. Masturbation can be an important addition to your sexual repertoire, not in competition to your sexual relationship with your partner, but in conjunction with it.

With practice, you can soon establish your own ritual of pleasures. Remember, it may not happen all at once, but getting there is half the fun. Once you learn how, you will wonder how you ever lived without it.

SENSATE FOCUS

Sensate focus simply means learning how to enjoy all the different skin-touch sensations that are not equated with raw sex. It is "expanded" touching. As a couple, take every opportunity to touch each other, consciously avoiding all the conventional erogenous zones (breasts and genitals). As you embrace each other, feel the softness, the warmth, the way your partner's body melds in around yours. Slowly and delicately trace your finger down your partner's forearm, hold their hand and gently tickle the palm, or stroke the back of their neck. Remember, there are no sexual messages, just the pleasure of body contact and touching.

Now, you may progress to a back rub. It is wonderful to set the scene—a candle, soft music—but no expectations of sex. You may ask for a back rub or you may offer one. Or you can flip a coin. There must be no expectation that "You give me a back rub and then I'll do you." The only rule is no hidden agenda for sex. Just relax and allow your body to enjoy all the pleasurable sensations. If there is one particular stroke or area that you enjoy more than others, tell your partner or gently take your partner's hand and guide it to the moves you enjoy. This is not being selfish; this is knowing what makes you feel good.

While you are giving a back rub, focus on different areas, different amounts of pressure, different movements—from "kneading" the muscles of the shoulder, upper arm or buttocks, to a gentle pitter-pat down the backbone. You may stroke with a piece of fur, a square of silk or satin. "Different strokes for different folks." Be innovative. Pour a little honey in his navel and lap it up, or simply kiss him all over. Just reading about it probably turns you on, and that is okay, too.

A back rub can progress to a foot massage, legs, arms, hands and chest. Avoid contact with breasts and genitals. This includes male breasts which are also an erogenous zone. Remember that just because you are aroused does not mean you have to do something about it.

Even with these injunctions, one or the other of you may become sexually aroused, and that is okay. Enjoy these feelings but, again, you do not do anything about it. The idea is to change the equation that touch equals sex. This is touch for pleasure. Period. If you are really feeling the need for relief, you may masturbate, although most therapists recommend that you wait till some other time when you are on your own. When you masturbate to ejaculation and/or orgasm then, it will not be as a direct result of arousal from touching your partner.

If working on sensate focus under the direction of a

therapist, he will suggest continuing this for a pre-scribed length of time, anywhere from one to two months. Then, when it is mutually agreeable, you progress to touching the breasts, not with the idea of sexual arousal as the goal, but pleasuring your partner. Gentle circular movements, stroking, gently touching the nipples, very tender squeezing. No rough stuff here. Most women dislike "heavy-handed" touch, re-gardless of what the porn magazines tell us. You may kiss the nipples, gently suck, "gumming," but abso-lutely no biting. Tell your partner what you like about their breasts: the size, the shape, the warmth, the way they respond to touch and the nipples become erect and "pokey."

If you are the recipient, do not even think about your partner getting bored or tired. Just enjoy yourself without feeling responsible. Allow your partner to con-tinue until they indicate, "that's it for now, dear. . . ."

If you are not feeling entirely comfortable, do not proceed to the next phase. Take time to get the most out of these sensate focus exercises.

If you both feel that you are ready to move on, then slowly and gradually move to the genitals. But go slowly. Remember your courtship days; when you were starting into "heavy petting" you did not simply make a grab for each other's genitals.

Explore your partner's body as if it were the first time. Run your fingers through the pubic hair, out to the groove in the groin up to the hips. Very lightly, allow your hand to rest on the genitals, and slowly move your whole hand back and forth. You may notice that your partner moves in rhythm with your hand. They may even lift their hips up and towards you, almost in a thrusting movement. This is wonderful, but do not rush it now. Again, arousal does not demand instant relief, neither of you will die of terminal "horniness."

Sensate focus puts the emphasis on pleasure, not on performance, proving the statement: "Getting there is half the fun." Once you have experimented and broadened your horizons, sex no longer needs to be boring and repetitious.

Sensate focus also takes the performance pressure out of sexual activity. Even if it does not result in a grand and glorious orgasm or ejaculation, all is not lost. Both of you had a pleasant time and enhanced the intimacy in your relationship.

Pleasuring

Some therapists recommend that you keep your hand over your partner's hand to guide your partner and indicate what type of touch you most enjoy. This gives you a sense of power and control and removes the pressure from your partner. No longer does the partner have the responsibility to anticipate exactly what would pleasure you.

If you become very aroused, then move their hand to another less responsive area till you feel ready to continue. This way you get to enjoy the ebb and flow of arousal and to learn that you can ease off—it will come back again. Both males and females can relax and enjoy this expanded and extended lovemaking.

When you both feel that you are ready for intercourse, proceed very slowly through the sensate focus exercises until you are both fully aroused. It is best if the male lies on his back and his partner slowly straddles him and allows her genitals to come in contact with his.

Just lie there with neither of you moving. Simply enjoy the closeness of your body contact. Slowly and gently guide the tip of the penis just barely into the vaginal opening. Remain motionless, enjoy the sensation from feeling his penis inserted, the throbbing pulsating sensation of the penis in the vagina. For the male, enjoy the gentle gripping of the vagina around the penis. Stay there, motionless, until the erection subsides. Then withdraw the penis and return to other forms of pleasurable touching.

Next time, the penis may be fully inserted into the vagina, but refrain from thrusting. Take time to observe and enjoy the sight of your bodies joined, but with no sense of urgency to get on with it. Stay relaxed and in control.

Always conclude each stage with loving touching, hugging, holding and stroking. If you are feeling desperate for sexual release, you may masturbate. Here you are re-learning that you can satisfy yourself. Your partner is not responsible for your satisfaction.

Once you have the sense of being in control, then you may begin lowering yourself up and down with his penis in your vagina. You may speed up or slow down as you would like, or perhaps in response to a signal from your partner. Communication is still essential here. Your partner cannot anticipate exactly what would please you right now, nor you him.

If you are ready to ejaculate or reach orgasm, it is now quite okay. And if it does not work this time, that's not devastating. Simply go back a few steps and begin slowly again.

This whole process will take several months or more. Do not rush it. It may have taken twelve years to find effective therapy; it takes time to allow it to work.

Unfortunately, most people experience their first sexual encounters in the "missionary position," male on top. Some reasons for this are modesty on the woman's part; she did not want him on the bottom, able to see her breasts, her body, and to see the penis entering the vagina. There is also a belief that if the woman is on top, it is not her "first time." She may feel cheap, sleazy (only prostitutes do *that!*).

But the position of female on top allows the woman to control the depth of thrusting and the speed. The male may also indicate what he would like at any given point.

You may also wish to experiment with different positions—side by side is very close and intimate and loving. Another is the "rear entry sex" (female on all fours on the bed, at the edge, head down, tush up). This position allows the male to stimulate her breasts and genitals manually, and she can reach back and stimulate his penis and testicles. Then very slowly and gently, the male can insert the penis in the vagina, making sure there is sufficient lubrication present. Thrust very gently, while continuing to stimulate each other. We call this "Fido and Fifi" position or "doggie style."

For many women, this position takes a little getting used to because she may feel self conscious about her tush being up in the air. And she may feel vulnerable, and even resent her partner being in such a position of power. Talk about your feelings with your partner.

This position is beneficial for women who have a

retroverted uterus (tilted back towards her backbone). The uterus falls forward in this position. Or if she has ovarian cysts and thrusting is painful in the missionary position, this allows the ovaries and cysts to slide forward out of the way. Many males find this position very exciting, new and different. "If you ain't tried it, don't knock it."

ORAL-GENITAL SEX

One of the chief obstacles to oral sex is that most people, males and females, feel that their genitals are ugly, although most of these people have never closely examined the genitals of anybody of the same sex.

> Dear Sue,
> My genitals are so ugly—the lips hang down and they are a dirty colour and all wrinkled and wet. I undress in the closet and I won't let my husband even look at me down there. How do I know if mine are normal?

This is not unusual. Many females have never even seen any pictures of female genitals, and, until relatively recently, there were no drawings, least of all coloured pictures, of female genitals in textbooks used for sex education.

Liking Female Genitals

Betty Dodson, who wrote *Sex for One*, is a controversial artist who is dedicated to informing women about their bodies and sexual responses. She has included an extensive collection of beautiful drawings of women's genitals. The book is invaluable for increasing your comfort level with your own body and your sexuality.

Because male genitals are external, most males are familiar with the appearance of their genitals during sexual arousal. But very few females are comfortable with using a mirror to look at their genitals during sexual arousal. This is most unfortunate because the changes are so dramatic and totally awesome. Many women are oblivious, for example, that their clitoris becomes erect when they are aroused. (We have described these changes in the section on masturbation.)

Most females, from pre-puberty on, are told that their genitals do not smell pleasant. In particular, it comes in the form of instruction about menstruation, to "practise good personal hygiene," "be sure to wash well" and "you should douche after menstruation to eliminate odours." There was a TV commercial along this line depicting a mother telling her daughter she wanted only the best for her. Bunkum.

Healthy genitals do not "smell bad." The vagina is a self-cleaning organ and the secretions keep the acid-alkaline balance to prevent infections. The discharge is the end result of this on-going cleansing. If a female does not have a bath or a shower fairly regularly, this discharge builds up, starts to break down and results in a distinctive "genital odour" that might be offensive.

Again, fresh menstrual blood has no odour any more than blood from a cut finger or a nose bleed has an odour. But if menstrual blood is exposed to air and body heat, it starts to deteriorate or break down, and then develops an unappealing odour. This washes away with a bath or a shower. I strongly advocate a return to the long, leisurely bath. When you stand under a shower, the secretions in the folds of the genitals might not be washed away, whereas if you plop your bottom in a tub of warm water, the discharge will all wash away, leaving you squeaky clean.

You do not have to use strong deodorant soaps, and I advise against using a "personal deodorant spray" or underarm deodorant spray. These contain perfumes and chemicals that can irritate the mucous membrane of your genitals, cause irritation and leave you vulnerable to other infections.

It is essential that we like our own genitals and feel good about them. They are unique for every woman, and to be enjoyed by us and our sexual partner. There will always be some males who are turned off by the appearance of female genitals, possibly based on fears of "captive penis." Some males are convinced that a woman's vagina will clamp down on his penis and he will be locked in there.

Liking Male Genitals

Males seem to be quite comfortable with their own genitals (except their testicles—males often don't like to touch or look at them), but many females have difficulty with male genitals. It seems to be easier for those who were raised with brothers, and those who have a good sex education at home and at school. When a woman is in a loving relationship in which there is tenderness and caring, she is more likely to become comfortable with oral-genital stimulation, such as kissing, licking, sucking and taking his penis into her mouth. I hate to say it, but it is an acquired taste, not something most females initiate at the beginning of a relationship.

Many females write telling me that they are scared they will "do something wrong." Relax, there is very little you can do wrong, especially if you and your partner are able to communicate to each other what he finds pleasurable. If it is not pleasurable, he can gently guide you to make the moves that feel good for him.

Myths about Oral Sex

Many people are uncomfortable with the idea of oral-genital sex because of their misconceptions. Let's clear up these myths about oral sex performed on a male (fellatio) or oral sex performed on a female (cunnilingus).

• Unless your partner has a sexually transmitted disease or is HIV positive (the AIDS virus), oral sex is safe.

• You cannot get pregnant from oral sex. If you are involved in genital to genital contact, not necessarily intercourse, you could possibly get pregnant, but not from oral sex. (You can get pregnant if he is sexually aroused, touches his penis and carries some of the lubrication or ejaculate to your genitals, perhaps inserting his fingers into your vagina. This fluid on his fingers could cause a pregnancy, unless you are using an effective method of contraception.)

• You will not get pregnant if you take ejaculate into your mouth and then spit it into a tissue; nor is there any way you can get pregnant if you swallow ejaculate. The digestive system and the reproductive system are entirely separate, so you are safe.

• You will not get fat if you choose to swallow

ejaculate. There are said to be only thirty-five calories in each ejaculation.

• Ejaculate will not cause nor clear up your acne. It does not matter if you rub it on your face or if you swallow it.

• Ejaculate does not contain vitamin E, so it will not keep you young. There is no conclusive evidence that vitamin E will keep you young.

• If you swallow ejaculate, or if you rub it on your chest, you will not develop big breasts.

• Swallowed ejaculate will not alleviate menstrual cramps, although pleasurable sex with orgasm can help relieve your monthly cramps.

• If your partner is not infected with HIV, you simply cannot get AIDS from oral sex.

• There are only two diseases you can get from oral sex with your partner (unless your partner is HIV positive): herpes or pharyngeal gonorrhea. So, if you have an outbreak of "cold sores" (herpes simplex 1) and you "go down" on your partner, your partner might get genital herpes 1. The fluid from the cold sore blister is loaded with the herpes 1 virus and you could infect him. If your partner has cold sores, even at the earliest prodromal stages, do not kiss them goodnight. You could get herpes and you will not appreciate it.

• Your partner will not become addicted to oral sex to the exclusion of other forms of sexual activity.

If you are involved in oral sex and your partner has gonorrhea, there is a possibility that the bacteria from the discharge from his urethra will get into your mouth. This could infect the glands at the back of your throat. About two to seven days later, you will notice that your throat is sore, swollen and there is a discharge. Go to your doctor immediately and until you have both been treated, abstain from kissing and sexual contact.

Oral Sex Performed on a Male

Now that we have put those myths to rest, we can work on becoming more comfortable with oral sex for both males and females.

> Dear Sue,
> My boyfriend likes oral sex and he is always nagging me to give him a blow job. I think it is sick. We have been together for two years now and I have only tried it twice and I hate it. He says it is only fair because he goes down on me and I really enjoy that. How can I develop a taste for it?

You can see his point. He cannot understand how she can enjoy receiving oral sex but can hate performing it. "What is sauce for the goose is sauce for the gander."

If you are not sure about oral sex, you may be reluctant to take the initiative. The key is to go slow. You may wish to incorporate oral sex as part of a massage or a back rub. Very gently, run your fingers through his pubic hair, allowing him time to enjoy the sensations. Then slowly move your hand down, touch his penis, gently stroke it and be aware how he becomes sexually aroused. The penis becomes erect, the foreskin retracts, the blood vessels are full and throbbing. In fact, his penis is pulsating. Observe how the penis has changed colour and has taken on a rosy red hue. Then slowly slide your hand down and caress his testicles. Notice how they are distended, have also changed colour and have pulled up quite tight to his body. They are very firm and throbbing.

Very unobtrusively, move your hand back from the testicles to the very sensitive area between the base of the penis and the rectum. This is also an erogenous zone.

Then you can start out by gently licking the tip of the penis, and gradually move down over the head of the penis and all along the shaft, right to the base. You may move back up and down in this manner, and then you may take the head of his penis in your mouth. Make certain that there is sufficient saliva there to reduce friction and discomfort. Do remember that the penis is very sensitive and can easily become sore and irritated.

You need to be aware that you do not take so much of the penis into your mouth that you hit the "gag reflex" that is at the back of your throat. You do not want to throw up, and retching will not make it pleasurable for either of you.

At this stage, you may wrap your hand around his penis. He will place his hand over yours to guide you as to pressure and firmness and speed. You may, slowly at first, move your hand up and down the shaft of the penis and gradually you will speed up.

Meanwhile, you may continue to lick and suck on the head of the penis, in rhythm to your hand movements. If you continue to stimulate him in this manner, you will be aware of the changes in his breathing pattern, the muscles of his body are very tense and in contraction. If the stimulation continues, he will ejaculate, then relax completely and enter the refractory phase.

Before you begin, you will have to be very clear how you feel about taking ejaculate into your mouth. If you have aversions to this, then you will have to arrange ahead of time that he will give you a signal when he is about to ejaculate. At this point, you take your mouth away, leaving lots of lubrication on his penis. Continue to stimulate him with your hand alone, until he ejaculates. This way he can ejaculate on his abdomen, not in your mouth.

If you do not mind ejaculate in your mouth, but you are not comfortable swallowing it, you will need to have a box of tissues close at hand. When he ejaculates in your mouth, you can spit it into the tissues to be disposed of later.

It really does break the "magic of the moment" if you immediately leap up, scramble off the bed, dash to the bathroom to spit the ejaculate into the toilet, followed by frantic flushing and cleaning your teeth and swishing with mouth wash, and you come back smelling like a sterile medicine cabinet. The message he might get from that is that you find his ejaculate repulsive, that you are simply doing it to please him, and personally, you can't stomach it. So if it is possible, avoid that scenario. Most women simply swallow the ejaculate and leave it at that.

Oral-genital sex can be a form of sexual foreplay and stimulation, and once he is very "turned on," you may move on to sexual intercourse, but only if you feel that you are ready. That wasn't so bad now, was it?

Oral Sex Performed on a Female

Oral sex on a female is much like that on a male. It is best done very slowly, gently and lovingly. After touching her genitals with a feather touch, stroke her clitoris, alternating with a slow, gentle, circular motion over the clitoris, continuing touching and petting down the labia and around the vaginal orifice. In all probability, there will be quite a bit of lubrication around her genitals. This lubrication tells you that she is enjoying the activity and she is becoming sexually aroused.

The male would probably begin by kissing around her genitals, then gently licking and sucking and kissing her clitoris. Some females find it very stimulating if he gently flicks his tongue over her clitoris.

You will note that the key word here is "gentleness." Manual or oral "grinding of her clitoris" is very painful and will turn her off very quickly. So, if she indicates that she would like something else, take her word for it.

Dear Sue,
When my husband and I have oral sex, he is very rough. Although I ask him to be gentle, it seems as if he wants to crawl right inside me; head, body, hands, all of him. Is this normal? I find it a real turn off.

If I could have a few words, I would say to him, "Gently, Bentley."

Some females find it very pleasurable if the male inserts two or three fingers into her vagina while he is kissing her clitoris. Then he can change tactics and kiss the vaginal opening, insert his tongue into her vagina while he is manually stroking her clitoris. Be innovative and flexible in your sexual repertoire.

As with the male, it is possible to kiss and lick her

perineum (the area around her genitals) including the area between the vagina and her rectum. This is very titillating.

As you are reading this, you are probably aware that you became quite sexually aroused. That is perfectly okay and normal, and if reading about it is exciting, imagine doing it. Wow!

But some people will never be comfortable with oral sex. No matter how their partner reassures them, they would never accept it or be involved in it. We just have to accept that, unless they are willing to talk to a therapist to help identify the block and work it through with counselling.

Oral sex is a very personal, intimate behaviour, and the trust level has to be very high for both partners to enjoy it. I do not want anybody to be involved in oral sex, unless they have decided to "give it a whirl." Nobody should be pressured into doing it to keep their partner happy.

Secrets About Men Every Woman Should Know by Barbara DeAngelis is a book that can help women understand the important role oral sex plays in sexual activity. This book also gives a lot of other insights into the male psyche. I only hope she writes a companion book for males about women.

SEXERCISES: KEGEL EXERCISES

Dear Sue,
I have two children, age seven and nine, and I am di-.
vorced. I have a new boyfriend and I don't think I am

*"tight" enough to suit him. Is there any surgery I can
have to snug up my vagina a bit?*

Yes, there is surgery that will cut out a section of the
vagina and stitch it up tighter. But it is surgery requir-
ing general anaesthetic and there are always risks with
any surgery. Most gynaecologists would prefer that you
get involved in safer, easier non-surgical therapy,
called the Kegel exercises. These exercises will help
you strengthen the muscles around your vagina.

Both males and females have a group of muscles
that are attached to the hip bones (pelvic bones), the
tail bones (coccyx) and to your pubic bone in the
front above the genitals. These are called pubococcygeal muscles or "PC" muscles for short. Think of
them as a "sling" that holds up all of your internal organs.

These muscles are always under pressure, but this is
increased dramatically during pregnancy or rapid
weight gain. They also become "atonic" (having loose
muscle tone) with aging, when the muscles relax and
become saggy. There may also be some loss of muscle
tone after lower abdominal surgery.

Some people inherit poor muscle tone, but if they
exercise on a regular basis, it is possible to strengthen
the muscles.

If the muscles cannot support your organs, they
may "prolapse" or hang down into the vagina. The
bladder may bulge into the vagina (a condition called
"cystocele"), the rectum may bulge into the vagina (a
condition called "rectocele", or the uterus may prolapse into the vagina. Each of these conditions requires surgical repair. So apart from improving your

sex life, the Kegel exercises benefit your general health and well-being.

There are another set of muscles, called sphincters, surrounding the rectum, the urethra (the little tube through which both males and females urinate), and the vaginal opening. These muscles may also lose tone during pregnancy. Sloppy rectal sphincters may contribute to hemorrhoids, which are veins close to the rectum, and may prolapse and protrude outside the body, causing severe discomfort, itching and pain.

"Stress incontinence" may also occur if the urethra prolapses and causes increased pressure that prevents the sphincter from contracting completely. If you laugh, sneeze, bend over, exercise strenuously or go jogging, even though your bladder is not full, you may not be able to stop the flow of urine and small spurts will be expelled. Very embarassing. Many people are forced to wear "mini pads" all the time, some even have to wear a form of adult diaper.

Kegel exercises may be done after surgery or the delivery of a baby, when you feel comfortable again. But they can also be done at any time to help get your pubococcygeal muscles back in shape again. It is never too late, you can start now, and it is so simple. You do not even have to get into sweat pants and runners. You can do these exercises anywhere—at the dining room table, when you are standing at the sink doing the dishes or stuck in traffic.

Exercising to strengthen all these muscles will improve a woman's sexual pleasure. She will be able to contract the PC muscles and the vaginal sphincter tighter around his penis, so she will be more aware of his penis in her vagina and the pleasurable sense of fullness. And by being able to grip the penis firmly, she will increase the pleasurable sensations for her partner.

These exercises will also increase vaginal lubrication in post-menopausal females, making sex more pleasurable for both partners and reducing the possibility of cystitis (bladder infection). Chronic cystitis may lead to scar tissue forming around the urethra, causing stress incontinence.

The Faucet

To begin with, you need to locate your PC muscles and establish how strong they are. To do this, simply sit on the toilet (yes, men too,), spread your legs apart, start urinating, then stop the flow of urine without squeezing your legs together. If you are not able to stop the flow, you need to start the exercises right then and there. Begin by stopping and starting the flow of urine every time you go to the bathroom. You will be amazed at how quickly you start to gain control. This is like turning a tap off and on.

The Wave

This exercise can be done anywhere, but for starters sit on a chair and slowly tighten all the PC muscles and sphincters, slowly, from back to front. Hold for a count of ten. Then slowly release, relax and repeat. Think of waves slowly rolling onto a beach and out again. If you get bored doing it in slow motion, you can do it rapidly, pull up and in, relax quickly and do it again. If you exaggerate this exercise it becomes a "push-pull" movement, causing the rectum to bulge, then pull up sharply. Some doctors recommend you do these exercises one hundred times a day. Every time you stop for a red light at an intersection, practise the Wave until the light changes to green. Do it while you are talking on the phone or sitting on a bus. The world does not need to know you are exercising your genitals. You can just sit there with a silly grin on your face.

Floor Exercises

If you are doing abdominal exercises on a regular basis, take a few moments and do some pubococcygeal exercises while you are down there. Lie on your back on the floor and raise your hips. Your weight will be resting on your head and feet. Pull in your PC muscles. Flop your knees apart and then together again, continuing to keep the muscles of your genital area contracted.

Basic "leg raises" also tighten the PC muscles around the genitals. Sit up straight with your back pressed against a wall, legs extended straight out in front of you. Raise and lower one leg twenty times. Then change legs and repeat. Gradually increase the number of leg raises until you can comfortably do fifty with each leg.

Abdominal exercises will also indirectly tone genital muscles, so crunches and sit-ups are beneficial too.

These exercises need to be done regularly to increase and maintain muscular strength and control. Most can be done while watching TV, or in bed before you fall asleep, or while waiting for the next course in a restaurant. Do them regularly and you will be amazed at the results.

Kegel Exercises for Men

Men can benefit from doing the same Kegel exercises.

Males who practise the Kegel exercises will gradually realize that it is possible to maintain control of their sexual excitement level. They will be able to delay ejaculation, thus extending the period of love-making and increasing their sexual satisfaction.

If a male practises Kegel exercises when he is masturbating by himself, he can stimulate himself almost to the point of ejaculation, contract the PC muscles then hold off. He will lose his erection, then restimulate himself. This way, he recognizes the pre-ejaculatory sensations, and is able to control ejaculation. This is a definite component of therapy for the problem of premature ejaculation. Kegel exercises can also strengthen males' urinary sphincter and prevent "dribbling" as they grow older.

PART II

• • •

WHEN YOUR
BODY LETS
YOU DOWN

CHAPTER 6

NOT TONIGHT, DEAR

• • •

LOW SEX DRIVE

Dear Sue,
I really try to get turned on. My partner tries every-
thing, but nothing works. I am just not interested and
I don't care if I never do it again. Sometimes I do it
just to keep my partner happy. I wasn't always like
this. I once had a boyfriend and we would spend the
whole weekend "doing it." Now I just grit my teeth
and try to fake some enthusiasm, but basically I feel
dead.

This letter could have been written by any number of
women because low sex drive (also called "Inhibited
Sexual Desire" (ISD) or "Desire Phase Dysfunction") is

such a common problem. Both sexes suffer from it equally, even though popular myth associates it mostly with women. Professionals define it as a specific psychosexual dysfunction caused by the lack of desire, which is a source of distress for the patient or the patient's partner.

If a person's level of sexual desire has always been low, they are diagnosed as "primary." Low sex drive is called "secondary" if sexual desire decreases significantly following a period of higher interest.

Problems arise in a relationship if there is a wide difference between the sexual drive of two partners. If the interest was normally high, followed by a dramatic decrease, the interpretation might be "You don't love me any more," or "You don't find me attractive any more," or "You are seeing someone else."

People generally believe that women have a lower sex drive than men. However, I am convinced that female sexual interest is just as high, but the difference is that women are socialized by spoken or unspoken attitudes, such as "a nice girl does not let on when she is horny." In actual fact, she may not even recognize the symptoms of sexual arousal.

It is estimated that about fifty percent of people who seek sex counselling present low sex drive as their initial complaint. Therapists estimate that about twenty percent of couples seeking relationship counselling complain of inhibited sexual desire as part of the problem.

A person's sex drive is never static; it is cyclical. It normally waxes and wanes throughout the life cycle and may be attributed to life circumstances. In any relationship, there are periods of close intimacy that generally include frequent sexual activity. And then there may be a normal period of withdrawal, a pulling away while each partner regains autonomy and individuality.

Unfortunately, we tend to regard the person who is not interested in sex as the "one with the problem." Actually, he or she would not say it was a problem but the other partner, who wants more sex and is expressing dissatisfaction, makes the LSD (low sex drive) partner feel abnormal. In reality, it is really the person with the normal sex drive who often has the problem. They are experiencing feelings of rejection, failure as a lover and frustration. So it becomes a "couple problem," and therapy would involve relationship and communication counselling, plus strategies to make sex more appealing to both partners.

Because there are no absolute "norms" for sexual activity, what is acceptable to one would be seen as "insatiable" to another and "total deprivation" to another. You can't pin it down. But you can find ways to accommodate for both ends of the spectrum of sexual desire.

Causes of Low Sex Drive

Dr. Lonnie Barbach, a noted sex therapist, has said, "Sexual desire is what leads you to the bedroom. Arousal is what happens when you get there." So there are two parts to the picture.

There are many reasons why people stay out of the bedroom when their sexual interest drops. Some of the reasons in the following list might ring a bell for you:

• Pregnancy, the after-effects of the birth of a baby,

premenstrual syndrome or a difficult menopause.

• Other body changes that make you feel unattractive.

• Any physical illness—a cold, heart attack, arthritis or surgery.

• Fatigue, exhaustion, stress or preoccupation with work or school.

• Frequent interruptions such as a crying baby, the phone ringing or even a late-night TV show.

• Medications such as tranquillizers, high blood pressure prescriptions, sleeping pills or birth control pills.

• Alcohol and "street drugs" such as marijuana or cocaine.

• Fear of pregnancy because of inadequate contraception or distrust of a partner's method of birth control.

• Dislike of the method of birth control you are using; for example some people dislike condoms.

• Fear of sexually transmitted diseases, especially with a new partner or if there is a suspicion that the other partner has been involved in another sexual relationship.

• Previous traumatic sexual experiences such as sexual assault (rape), battering or incest.

• Ignorance about sex, lack of information or lack of past experience.

• Early upbringing, extreme religious injunctions, negative attitudes and values about sex received from family, including disgust or revulsion, and the old Victorian idea that nice women do not enjoy sex. They only do it out of "marital duty"—"Just lie there and think of England."

- Depression or anxiety.
- Boredom, embarrassment, guilt or shame.
- Getting sex outside the relationship through an "affair" or from a prostitute.
- Severe relationship problems—no love, no intimacy, no communication.
- Over-intimacy. One partner needs greater distance and then develops low sex drive when the other partner does not back off.

Focus on the Relationship

All sex therapists will tell you that low sex drive is *the* most common problem they see in their practices. While it does occur in happy, well-adjusted relationships, couples who experience conflict and seek therapy for the dysfunction find that most of the focus of the therapy is on the relationship. There are some common causes of discord in a relationship:

- Anger and resentment built up over a period of time, the result of unresolved conflict—over such issues as equal division of household chores, money, outside friends and activities, family involvement, religion, job demands.
- Lack of intimate contact, close communications, hugging, holding and kissing, expressions of love, other than those that are sexual. (So often I hear, "The only time he ever touches me is when *he* wants sex" or "I am afraid to just give him a hug. He immediately interprets it as a sexual overture. All I wanted was to snuggle.")
- Power and control or "game playing" ("You went out with the boys, so I'll be damned if I am going to let you think I am interested in sex. I am going to punish you.)

• Need for a little bit of breathing space if the relationship is "enmeshed" and the partners are suffering from over-exposure to each other.

• Having grown up in a family that did not express love and affection, so that expressing love and caring through sexual contact is not something that just comes naturally.

Here are some aspects of your relationships for you to explore together with your partner:

• How frequently are you aware that you are interested in sex?

• How frequently do you actually have sex? Who initiates it and how do you feel about that? Who indicates disinterest and how do you let your partner know it is "no go"?

• How is the disinterest received?

• Do you have sexual fantasies? Does your partner have fantasies that you know of? Do you share them? Do you incorporate them in your lovemaking?

• Do you frequently masturbate alone? Does your partner masturbate? Is it pleasurable? (This will give you an idea of whether there is sexual arousal and an interest in sex. If there is sexual arousal and pleasure from masturbation, that generally tells us that the problem is in the relationship.)

Once we have these answers, then we can start working on improving the communications and developing problem-solving skills.

Medical Treatment and Therapy for Low Sex Drive

Therapy for low sex drive is more complicated than for any other sexual problem. It takes longer and the success rate of cures is not impressive. Sorry, but we must be realistic.

Each couple is unique, so there is no guaranteed magical therapy. Frequently, by the time the couple seeks out a therapist, much of the damage has been done. Anger and resentment have already built up. Both partners must be determined to work this out and be willing to change their communication styles. They need to spend more time being intimate and loving and settle all the conflicts that have piled up in the "scarbage bag." Otherwise the therapy won't be successful.

If your doctor or therapist suspects that the low sex drive is based on a medical problem, you may be given a complete physical examination and a few blood tests to give the doctor a full hormone profile.

If low sexual desire is caused by birth control pills, the doctor can change the contraceptive prescription. For low sex drive related to male climacteric or menopause, hormone therapy might be suggested. Some doctors will prescribe monthly injections of testosterone to females who are experiencing inhibited sexual desire. If there are other physical causes such as pain or a sexual dysfunction, such as premature ejaculation or vaginismus, treatment should be prescribed immediately. Your doctor may also have treatments to suggest for post-partum and post-operative patients. Medication and/or therapy for depression and stress management may be recommended for low sex drive. If the problem is based on a dysfunctional relationship, marriage and family counselling will be beneficial.

But I must warn you—many couples have a great deal invested in perpetuating this dysfunction. It gives them a sense of power and control. For this reason, utmost honesty is an essential for successful therapy.

Ideas for Self-Help

If you and your partner are "stuck" and cannot find a therapist, or while you are waiting for your first appointment and even while you are seeing a therapist, there are some things you can do to help yourselves.

Read together and aloud the sections in this book on "Touch," "Communication" and "Fantasy" (see pages 31-45 and 85-91). After that, there are other simple things you can do:

• Take time to be alone together and comfortable with each other.

• Do fun things together—go for a picnic, a hike a walk. But don't make it a chore.

• Hold hands and establish body contact with no sexual expectations.

• Avoid and try to reduce the stress levels in your life and avoid fatigue.

• Treat each other to a massage.

• Have a candlelight bubble bath together; be innovative and playful, tender and loving.

• Discuss your early upbringing and your attitudes about sex.

• Discuss any sexual traumas that might have had a negative effect.

• Discuss any relationship problems you can think of that might affect sexual desire.

• Take turns playing out your sexual fantasies.

• Remember, relationships flourish in response to the "three As": acceptance, approval and appreciation—and add a little adoration for good luck.

There will be times when your partner is interested in sex and you are just not enthusiastic at all. You could very gently, simply, say to your partner, "I will be there for you with love, but please do not expect passion tonight."

I am not suggesting that you "fake it," but that you please and pleasure and satisfy your partner. And you may find that once you get involved, you might enjoy it. It could be pleasurable and fun. Or it might even be a grand and glorious sexual romp. Some couples have even found that if they begin by "pretending" that they are turned on and just let it happen, before they know it they are aroused and loving it.

We do know that the less you have sex, the less you want and need sex. Once you get started again, you will be more interested the next time and before too long, *you* may be initiating the sexual activity, enjoying it, yes, even loving it. Sex is cerebral. The biggest sex organ you have is right between your two ears.

Let go and be a little innovative. Try it at noon, instead of Friday night after the news with the lights off. Try it in a sleeping bag, in front of the fireplace, or out on your balcony. If the black lace nightie loses its appeal, play the role of a "hooker" and insist he "leave the money on the night table." Allow your fantasies to surface and have fun with them.

But to do this, you have to feel good about yourself and your partner, like each other, and be relaxed and ready to enjoy.

Low Sex Drive in Males

We have the idea that all males have an "ever-ready penis"—up and at 'em every chance you get. But it just ain't so. The appetite for sex, the interest in sex, the need for sex all differ from person to person, just as the appetite for food does.

Sexual desire also has its quiescent periods. But it can be devastating for a male to compare his sex urge to other males and find that on a scale of one to ten, he ranks a low two-point-five. He may feel cheated, angry and resentful. He may also feel that he is abnormal, "not all man," or perhaps he may feel he has not found the right female to keep him turned on night and day.

Not only does the libido (a person's sex drive) differ from person to person, but there are stages in a male's life when he is very interested in sex, and times when it is the last thing on his mind. What scares males the most is hearing that a man is "in his prime" in his teens, and by the time he is twenty years old, he is on a downhill run, the best is behind him, game over, forget it. . . . So if he had a low sex drive to begin with or if he is a "late bloomer"—and this does happen—then he tends to either give up and regard any interest in sex as a "false alarm," or he hurries off to the doctor to see if a shot of testosterone would help.

While we are on the topic of testosterone, let me tell you, most physicians will not prescribe testosterone for low sex drive or any other perceived sexual dysfunction. Research has shown that testosterone may work for a few months, but the effect is basically psychological

—you think it works, so it works. As I said before, the biggest sex organ you have is between your two ears.

If you end up at the doctor's office asking for testosterone, your doctor should take the opportunity to talk about your low sex drive, to do a sexual history to find out if, in fact, there is a physical problem. The doctor's questions should include most of the following:

• Do you have sexual thoughts during the day? Do you enjoy them or do you feel guilty about them? Are they about your present partner, about anybody else, or just anyone passing by? Do you develop these thoughts into sexual fantasies?

• Do you have spontaneous erections?

• Do you masturbate to ejaculation? Is that pleasurable? How often?

• Do you engage in sexual intercourse? Who initiates it? If it is your partner, do you respond. If you are just not interested in sex, how does your partner handle it? Does she feel rejected? ("You don't love me," or "You don't find me sexy any more.") Or does she put you down? ("What's wrong with you? Other guys. . . .")

The doctor should also ask questions to uncover whether you are suffering from depression. People who are depressed and sad are seldom interested in sex. If depression seems to be your problem, you may be referred to a psychiatrist or psychologist for therapy to overcome the depression.

The doctor would also likely do a physical examination to make sure that there are no medical problems or physical abnormalities causing a low sex drive. This would include a blood test to determine your hormone profile or any endocrine disorders. The examination would also include an analysis of your nutrition, weight and exercise.

Your relationship with your partner is crucial if you suffer from low sex drive. You may think you have a low sex drive, but in fact your partner may not enjoy sex or may find sex painful, and so you lose interest.

For some males, "sublimation" is a factor—the unconscious mental mechanism you use to redirect your interest in sex towards other socially or morally acceptable activities such as work or sports. Everybody sublimates sexual urges to some degree, but if it is seriously interfering with your sex drive, then you need to explore your thoughts and feelings.

Becoming a Father

> Dear Sue,
> I can't understand what is happening, but ever since my wife got pregnant, I just could not think of her in a sexual way. So, I lied and said that I was scared that sex would harm the baby. Now the baby is six months old, and I love my wife but I just cannot bring myself to get sexual with her. Help! Our marriage is in deep trouble.

When your partner gets pregnant, life will never be the same again. There is a subtle but major shift. She is going to be the mother of your children and that changes the dynamics of your relationship.

Psychologists call it the "madonna-bitch complex," a shift away from regarding her as sexy, spontaneous, fun to have a sexual "romp" with. Once she is pregnant, she becomes the madonna, up on a pedestal, and you may see her as pure and untouchable. So you feel it is not "proper" to have uproarious, unbridled, sexual activity with her. That is something you do with "sleazy" ladies, but not with the mother of your children. Your partner may not be aware of this shift, so she takes it as a rejection: "Ever since I got pregnant, we don't fool around like we used to. . . ."

Males may also believe some myths about sex during pregnancy. They may think that vigorous sex might cause a spontaneous miscarriage or abortion, that it might be uncomfortable for her and hurt her or the baby. Some males find that a woman's changing body is not appealing. Other males really believe that their partner might get pregnant again and have another baby two months after the first is born. We may know that will not happen, but fear is often irrational.

As the pregnancy progresses, you have to be innovative to overcome what you see as an "obstacle." As one male said to me, "You can either kiss her or screw her, but you can't do both at the same time."

As a woman approaches "term" (delivery) she may be advised not to have intercourse. Some doctors are concerned that the uterine contractions during orgasm could trigger premature labour. Most males are willing to put intercourse on hold till after the baby is born.

Immediately after delivery, she may not be too "gung-ho" on intercourse for a period of time. The reasons are valid; her genitals will be sore and tender. If she has had an episiotomy (incision into the opening of the vagina to facilitate birth), it will take as long as a month before that is healed and comfortable. After that, there will be another period of time when her genitals will have a reduced sensitivity to sexual stimulation. The lochia, (vaginal discharge after birth) can be a bit off-putting for a few weeks after delivery and her breasts may be uncomfortable. Because of hormone fluctuations, she may have a low sex drive till her cycle gets back to normal again. Both partners may be concerned about adequate contraception, so abstaining is a good idea until you are sure you are protected.

This does not mean she does not want to be held, cuddled, hugged, stroked and touched, provided the implication is not that it will lead to intercourse.

Some males do not want to be involved with the birthing process, but our society makes a male feel he is abandoning his partner if he does not attend pre-natal classes and hang in there through the stages of labour and in the delivery room. But, as he watches her in pain, he may feel "I did this to her. I put her through this."

All these experiences may also alter his attitudes toward sex and intercourse. Observing the baby being delivered may change how he feels about her genitals, and when the baby comes home, he may feel displaced by the amount of attention his partner pays to the baby. He may even feel rejected, jealous and left out, and may try to compete with the baby for attention. Even when he and his partner are alone and intimate, he may feel that she is "not all there," that she always has one ear cocked for the baby, and he knows she is exhausted from looking after the newborn. So he is reluctant to initiate sex, delaying and hoping it will all get better. Meanwhile abstinence becomes the pattern and may well develop into a desire phase dysfunction. In one study of 126 couples, the response showed that sixty percent were having sex much less frequently than before the birth of their baby.

So, what do you do about it? Well, back to basics: communication. Talk about your feelings, listen to her feelings, understand and be aware. If you are sensitive to your partner's feelings, you can make a special effort to compromise in a way that satisfies both of you. Try to have "together time" when you can be intimate, not necessarily sexual but close and connected.

Males can always go back to "square one" and masturbate. This will keep your interest up, and it will take a lot of pressure off her, if she knows you are not dying of frustration and are capable of looking after yourself. That way, she does not have reason to feel resentful because she has to "service" you, too.

If you can survive this, you are well on the road to getting it together again. Becoming parents adds new aspects to building a close relationship with your partner.

LOW SEX DRIVE IN FEMALES

Pregnancy

Many couples have a very satisfactory sex life before the first pregnancy. Then she becomes pregnant and things start to change.

It is estimated that after a baby's delivery, forty-three percent of women desired less sex, whereas eighty-five percent of males said their sex drive was unchanged. Some couples seem to be aware of the changes and adapt, so they experience only a temporary slow-down.

Other couples feel just as sexy and horny during pregnancy and after delivery, and they continue to enjoy sexual activity.

However, women talk about a variety of effects of pregnancy, most of them relating to their sexual relationships:

• Exhaustion. This may be the first sign of pregnancy, and she just wants to sleep all the time. She may be suffering from morning sickness. Her breasts may be tender and sore.

• A change and fluctuation in hormone levels, resulting in a lack of sexual interest.

• Changes in body appearance: full, heavy breasts and stretch marks; the disapperance of her waistline, swollen ankles and fingers; a change in the genitals from a rosy pink colour to a dusky mauve or purple.

• A feeling of awkwardness resulting in not being able to bend over, and even a feeling of anger and resentment at having to "tote this great bulge around."

• Frequency of urination. She will have to urinate every hour, and will not feel "relieved" after a trip to the bathroom.

• Hemorrhoids from the pressure of the uterus on the rectum or from constipation or diarrhea.

Not a pretty picture, eh?

On top of that, there are psychological factors that may impede coitus. Some women who have never enjoyed sex figure that once they are pregnant, they have done their duty. Other women have cultural beliefs that make them avoid sex during pregnancy. Still others who have had problems becoming pregnant have fears that sexual activity could cause a miscarriage or premature labour and delivery. Some women may also have an uncomfortable feeling that the "baby is watching us do it" and may be traumatized by it.

After pregnancy

Some women absolutely blossom during pregnancy and after the birth of the baby. They feel like the ultimate female. Other women are just not prepared to accept the changes in their body and resent the pendulous breasts, the flab on the abdomen, and the residual fat that is so difficult to lose. They feel their body has been battered by the baby. Is it any wonder if they do not feel sexy?

> *Dear Sue,*
> *Motherhood sucks! My baby is eight months old and I don't give a damn if I ever "do it" again.*
> *After he was born, I cried for three days. I'm better now, but sometimes I resent this kid taking so much time and energy. Then I feel guilty about it. He did not ask to be born and it's not his fault. Other times I cope very well and enjoy him. But I dread this high-low feeling.*

After the baby is born it may take six to eight months before her hormone levels settle down, which may cause mood swings. If she is breast feeding, it may take longer. Her interest may be high one day and bottom out the next day. She may feel like an emotional yo-yo.

Also, after giving birth there is a dark red-brown vaginal discharge (lochia) that may last as long as a month. During this time tampons should not be used because of the risk of infection, but sanitary napkins are uncomfortable and irritating to the genitals and suture line. Many women, concerned about the increased risk of a vaginal infection or cystitis (a bladder infection) immediately after pregnancy may prefer to pospone sexual activity until things are back to normal.

If the delivery was difficult, particularly painful, or if there was an extensive episiotomy or surgical repair of a tear, intercourse may be uncomfortable for as long as two months until healing is complete. The episiotomy scar will have reduced sensitivity and may be numb and not respond to stimulation. In that case, a woman would definitely prefer a warm bath and a massage to having intercourse.

Breast feeding adds a whole new twist. The breasts may be tender and the nipples sore, and they may leak milk with the slightest touch or pressure. Damp . . . There may also be the feeling that you are taking food from the baby.

The new mother may be inexperienced in parenting and under a great deal of stress—not to mention exhaustion—after a few days of trying to meet the never-ending demands of a newborn. She just gets the baby settled, and there is her partner wanting sex. Just one more person she has to look after, before she can finally get some rest for herself.

Fear of another pregnancy shortly after birth might deter many women from wanting sex. If she is breastfeeding, she will not be prescribed the birth control pill, and a diaphragm is tricky immediately post-partum because the cervix is still enlarged and the vaginal opening may be sensitive. So the best contraceptive may be condoms and foam, used together every time.

She may also feel unappealing and unappreciated.

With the emphasis in the media on the "right" body shape, a woman can hardly help feeling "ugly" after giving birth. Finances may be tight, so she might not be able to afford stylish clothes that fit her new shape after the baby is born. Together, these add to a reduced self-image. It is easy to get lost in the mothering process.

However, there are things you can do for yourself. A new mother should make sure she gets a little extra rest each day to avoid being exhausted. It is easy to feel inadequate when you are exhausted. Forget about dusting the furniture. Have a nap instead.

And don't be bashful about accepting help. If your mother-in-law offers to help, suggest a casserole would be nice. Give up on the "super-mom" mentality. Make up a job list with your partner, go through the list and eliminate all but the essential ones for the time being. Then you can divvy them up, making sure that you both care for the baby as well as doing the dishes.

Make time for yourself. Eat smart and exercise regularly. You may want to join an exercise class for an hour every week. Spend a half-an-hour reading in the middle of the day. Even on a low budget, you can bargain shop for a few clothes that you can mix and match. Do something special for yourself every day. Think: "This I do for me."

Realistic Expectations

Low sex drive is not a new phenomenon. It has been part of people's experience for ages. But until recently, it was considered normal, and, as such, was simply accepted—"That's life, folks."

Now we have unrealistically high expectations of the

role of sex. It must be spectacular, sensational, and anything less is unacceptable. We have zero tolerance for less than the best. We also expect that the great hot passion we felt for our partners in the beginning of the relationship will last forever. We are not willing to settle for the inevitable change into compassionate love—gentle and tender, trusting and comfortable. When our partners do not live up to our expectations, we feel disappointed. Combined with this some anger and resentment over unresolved conflict, and the sexual activity drops off dramatically.

If couples start therapy before the disinterest in sex becomes an ingrained pattern, it is relatively easy to solve the problem of low sex drive. If it is a long-standing condition, then it will take longer to get to the bottom and work your way up to feeling good about yourself and your relationship.

CHAPTER 7

THE EARTH DIDN'T MOVE

• • •

DIDJA CUM?—THE ORGASM MYTH

Dear Sue,
I love my boyfriend and I enjoy sex, but I can't have
orgasms. I get all excited and wet, but I get to a cer-
tain point and then—poof—the excitement is gone.

Dear Sue,
I have never had an orgasm with my boyfriend. I can
by myself, but when I'm with my boyfriend, I am
afraid I'll look ugly, make noises or he'll think I'm a
slut. How can I get over this mental block?

Until relatively recently, no one would have written letters like this. Nobody, especially a woman, was supposed to work at enjoying sex. Sex was chiefly for procreation, rather than for pleasure. Women often tolerated it only because it was their wifely duty to keep their husbands from wandering, and men did it to reduce sexual tension and frustration.

After the First World War, we began to see articles in magazines with titles such as "How to Keep Your Husband Happy." Suddenly women began publicly to admit to getting some enjoyment out of sex, and men consciously began to try and "please the little woman." It soon became *de rigueur* for both males and females to have an orgasm every time they had sex.

The implication was that if you were a good lover you sexually satisfied your partner, which in turn became a responsibility: "If you love me, you would please me." Unfortunately, we did not know enough about human sexual responses nor did we encourage people to fantasize, masturbate and be responsible for their own sexual satisfaction first. Your partner was supposed to know intuitively exactly what would turn you on, and it had to work every time.

Women were unable to dump many of the old injunctions, but they were still expected to be the "last of the Red Hot Mamas." When they weren't the "Mamas" they were supposed to be, they were classified as "frigid," even in medical terminology.

Let's look at some of the myths about orgasm that are so common today:

• You are not a "real woman" until you have had an orgasm.

• You should have at least one orgasm every time

you have any sexual activity.

• Orgasms are triggered only by the penis thrusting in the vagina.

• A good lover will know intuitively how to bring all women, every woman, to orgasm.

• Males can always tell if a woman has had an orgasm.

• A "vaginal" orgasm is better than a "clitoral" orgasm.

• If a female does not have orgasms regularly, she will be frustrated and cranky.

• A female who has never had a baby will reach orgasm more easily than a woman whose vagina is stretched.

• A male with a big penis will bring a woman to orgasm much better than a guy with a small penis.

• Practise and concentration will help you get it right.

• Women who bring themselves to orgasm through masturbation never have an orgasm with a partner.

• Women should be able to have multiple orgasms.

As you read through this chapter, you will realize how these myths and misconceptions have influenced our attitudes towards sexual performance. Too often, they have really inhibited our enjoyment and have resulted in a great deal of performance anxiety as well as feelings of inadequacy and failure.

There's More than One Way

Very few women reach orgasm through sexual intercourse alone. Orgasms are the result of clitoral stimulation. Generally, penis thrusting in the vagina does not provide enough stimulation.

Research shows that about seventy percent of women do not reach orgasm with intercourse alone. But for some women, deep thrusting (down and back) does pull the clitoral hood (labia) down over the top of the clitoris with each thrust, and this provides the necessary stimulation. So if that works for you, great, but not to worry if it isn't happening that way.

Many, many women reach orgasm through a combination of cunnilingus (oral-genital sex on the female) and manual stimulation at the same time. That translates into: He gently sucks or licks your clitoris and at the same time gently inserts two or three fingers into your vagina and moves them around or mimics thrusting. Now reverse the procedure. He inserts his tongue into your vagina, while gently stroking or manipulating your clitoris.

And while we are at it, let's talk positions that are the most successful for female orgasm. The old reliable missionary position ranks low on the totem pole. Experiment and find what works best for you. Remember, getting there is half the fun.

Female on top seems to have the highest success rate. So, your partner lies on his back and when you are ready, you straddle his pelvis, your weight on your knees and toes. Now gently insert his penis into your vagina, just the tip, and be aware of the wonderful throbbing. As you gradually lower yourself onto his penis, he has two free hands to fondle your breasts, nipples, and certainly, last but not least, your clitoris.

Be sure there is sufficient lubrication, either your natural mucous secretions, saliva, Lubifax or KY Jelly. This way, you can control the depth of thrusting, get the necessary stimulation and the pleasure of seeing your two bodies joined.

Another position many couples find exciting and which provides a different prospectus is rear entry. I am not talking about rectal or anal sex here. The female crouches on her knees and elbows, backside up in the air. In this position, the male can touch and kiss her genitals from above or below. Then he gently inserts his penis into her vagina, slowly and gently thrusting in and out. He can lean forward, support himself on one hand, and with the other stimulate her breasts, then down and between her legs and commence clitoral stimulation. She meanwhile can reach through and stroke his testicles, the area around his rectum and the base of his penis. They can both get off on that one.

Dear Sue,
I was never able to reach orgasm, until we started to have sex with me on top. Then, bang, it happens every time. We call it "riding high." How come nobody ever tells you these things?

It's Not Up to Him

Women's magazines have exaggerated the importance of a male being responsible for a female partner to have a "big O" every time they have sex. Men have just accepted this, absolving women of any responsibility in helping themselves reach orgasm.

Because males still cling to the double myths that females need a "penis in vagina" (preferably a big penis) to have an orgasm and that females do not masturbate—so they are unable to sexually satisfy themselves—it's all up to the guys to do it and do it right.

The sad story is that many females have bought into the myths too, so they never learn to masturbate, never learn what is sexually satisfying for themselves. Please read the section on "Masturbation" (see page 95). Then examine your attitudes and values and decide if they are still valid in light of new information.

Dear Sue,
One morning I woke up and I was really feeling wet and horny, so in a half-asleep fog, I began to stroke my genitals. Boy, before too long, I was wide awake and zinging. My first orgasm and all by myself. What a feeling of power. "I am woman; hear me roar."

Once you get the straight facts, the anxiety and performance pressures seem to recede and things seem to fit into place. Ignorance is definitely not bliss.

Let Him Know What You Like

Before your proceed any further, be certain that both you and your partner have practised the communication skills outlined in Chapter 2 (see page 21). Now, you can very gently and in a non-threatening way tell your partner what kind of touching you would like, where and when. Simple statements such as "I really like it when you do that," or "mmmmm, that feels so good." Guide his hand to where you want to be touched; keep your hand over his and indicate the motion that is most pleasurable for you. Then say something like "Wow, that is marvellous. Just perfect. . . ."

It is okay to indicate that you prefer a feather touch and that clitoral grinding just does not do it for you. And if you want to touch yourself at the same time, that is acceptable too. Remember he has only two hands. You are not saying he is inept as a lover, just that you would like this too, and you are quite capable of helping yourself to pleasure. This is not something "he does for you," this is something you do together.

> *Dear Sue,*
> *At first my boyfriend was really upset when I would help him stimulate me. He said, "You don't need me," and "If you are so damn smart, do it yourself." But when I explained that it felt so good when we did it together, he relaxed and now it's wonderful. But it was scary for both of us at first.*

PHASES OF FEMALE ORGASM

Orgasm is defined as the climax of lovemaking, the explosive discharge of the accumulated tensions of the body's blood vessels and muscles. It is the experience of reaching the peak of sexual arousal and excitement.

Orgasm is an individual experience, it is unique for each person. There is no right or wrong way to experience orgasm since no two people respond the same way to the same stimuli.

Women who never reached orgasm used to be labelled "frigid." We now know that there is no such thing as a frigid female. All women are capable of orgasm if they are healthy, have no physical abnormalities and are knowledgeable about themselves as sexual human beings. A name we used to apply to females who had never had an orgasm was "anorgasmic." This name implied that the female was lacking, inadequate, inexperienced or missing out on something. Therapists now use the term "preorgasmic," meaning the person has never yet reached orgasm, but is capable of achieving one and is working towards becoming orgasmic.

There are four phases to orgasm. If you understand what is happening in the progression from one phase to the other, it is easier to understand where there can be interruptions.

The Excitement Phase

In the first phase, there are specific signs of sexual arousal:

• The mucous membranes of the mouth become engorged; the lips become fuller and moist.

• The breathing pattern changes to become heavier with short panting, gasping intakes of air; the pulse rate increases and the blood pressure rises.

• A red "sex flush" appears on the neck and chest.

• There is a forward pelvic thrusting movement, almost in a rhythmic movement, mimicking the thrusting of intercourse.

• The mucous membrane of the vagina becomes engorged. It feels swollen and throbbing.

• The clitoris protrudes from under the *labia minora* and literally becomes erect like a penis.

• An increase in vaginal secretions occurs. The vagina becomes very moist, damp, and even wet.

• The uterus becomes enlarged and almost rises up in the abdomen.

• The nipples become erect, enlarged and responsive to touch.

The Plateau Phase

• The vagina becomes more wet with increased lubrication.

• The sex flush extends to the face.

• Breathing becomes faster and shallow; the heart rate and blood pressure increase.

• Sensations level off, consolidate, almost go on hold.

Orgasm Phase

> *Dear Sue,*
> *What does an orgasm feel like? I am not sure if I have ever had one. How do you know for sure what is happening?*

I think the best way to answer that question would be to quote from some of the many letters I have received from women describing the sensations and emotions they experienced during orgasm:

• A restless, frantic or frenzied feeling. (You know you want more of the same.)

• A sense of "desperate gripping," pulling your partner toward you, clutching your partner.

• Rhythmic contractions of the pubococcygeal muscles in the pelvic floor; the vaginal walls contract as well as the rectal sphincter.

• The body trembles and shakes, and the muscles

go into spasm. (Women describe it as "quivering all over.")

• There is a sense of explosion, "over the top." Boom!

It seems to be almost like trying to describe what a sneeze feels like. My correspondents struggled to describe what they felt at the time of orgasm:

• "Not only was it incredible at the moment, there was a feeling of power: I am woman; I can do anything."

• "I was filled with confidence and enthusiasm."

• "I had a sense of togetherness, connectedness, oneness."

• "I wanted to have sex with him again, to do it all over again."

• "I felt a weakness, lightheadedness, head pounding, hot blood coursing through my veins."

• "I had a sense of being finished, relaxed, released and relieved."

• "I was aware of decreasing contractions of my genitals, and the spasms ceased."

• "I felt connected with my partner, close and intimate."

The Refractory Phase

This is the last phase of orgasm and can be described as follows:

• You feel a sense of total relaxation and release, a weak and wobbly feeling.

• There is a sense of intimacy, connectedness, oneness and unity with your partner.

• You may feel completely "satiated," although many women can easily be restimulated to have another orgasm.

• Eventually, you return to normal breathing, with a normal heart rate.

• You feel very relaxed and some couples like to cuddle and fall asleep; others seem to need a bit of space and gradually fall asleep close but not touching.

BLOCKS TO ORGASM

Physical Blocks to Female Orgasm

There are many reasons why women experience difficulty reaching orgasm. Some of them are psychological and some are purely physical. Let's take a look at some of the physical blocks:

• Exhaustion, fatigue, or aches and pains such as arthritis, headache or hemorrhoids.

• Vaginal infections such as yeast, herpes, trichomonas or chlamydia, causing tenderness and irritation of the genitals and intense discomfort.

• Insufficient lubrication, dryness of the genitals.

• Medication causing low sex drive, such as tranquillizers, sedatives, medication for high blood pressure.

• Pain because of recent childbirth, episiotomy repair or surgery.

• Advanced stage of pregnancy.

• Ovarian cysts, endometriosis, retroverted uterus, pelvic inflammatory disease (PID).

• Constipation with impacted feces making vaginal stimulation uncomfortable.

• Alcohol or street drugs, such as "pot," causing low sex drive.

• Bladder infection causing frequent urination.

Psychological Blocks to Female Orgasm

- Fear of pregnancy or STDs.
- Sex in a hurry—"quicky sex"—with insufficient foreplay and time to become sexually aroused.
- Lack of privacy, fear of being heard, discovered or interrupted (baby due to wake up; parents coming home early).
- Lack of romance and wooing, or an unappealing or uncomfortable location.
- Unresolved conflict in the relationship.
- Preoccupation with outside factors, such as work, money, in-laws or children.
- Guilt, shame, embarrassment or lack of knowledge.
- Lack of self-concept and self-esteem: "I am not good enough."
- Boredom. Sexual activity with the same partner may fall into monotonous, repetitious and downright dull habits.

Unrealistic expectations can in themselves be a mental block to orgasm.

There is a great deal of pressure on women to be orgasmic in order to be a "complete woman." Women also have the feeling that orgasm is something they should "do" for their partner. Many women feel pressured to have orgasms to convince their partner that he is a good lover—if she is not reaching orgasm, he will feel it is his fault, that he must be doing something wrong or his penis is too small. Occasionally women experience peer pressure from their friends when the conversation turns to sex and everybody else seems to be able to do it and she hasn't yet "got there." It's regarded as a sign of sexual maturity.

Fear is probably the biggest block of them all. Here are some varieties:

• Fear of losing control ("I am afraid I will flip out" or "I will get hooked on it; then I will become a nymphomaniac, insatiable").

• Fear of losing bladder control and wetting the bed.

• Fear of making noise, of having "vaginal farts" or of moaning and groaning or of saying something "unlady-like" such as "More, more, more" or, even worse, "Fuck me good." Even something as simple as the bed squeaking to a distinctive beat makes some women nervous.

These fears are based on misinformation and misconceptions of what is normal and acceptable in female sexual responses. They tie in with our image of ourselves as a "proper lady" and our notion of "nice women don't do things like that." So, to us, doing it appears cheap, sleazy, animalistic, and oversexed.

After you identify your fears and anxieties, it is important to determine if you are being intimidated and blocked by any of them. Accept only accurate information, check out your reactions with your partner. Then let your fears go. Easier said than done. However, your fears may prevent you from getting what you want and deserve out of sex. You can do it.

You may be very self-conscious of what you perceive as your body inadequacies. You may think you look ugly in a contorted position with your legs up around your ears or with you on top so that he can see your "droopy" breasts.

You may feel that your genitals "don't smell very good" or "They look gross, all wet and gooey."

However, this is what makes you female.

Of course, how you see your body is closely related to your self-image, which plays a powerful role in your sexual responses. If you do not like your body, it is difficult to understand how your partner can possibly like your body.

Although it does not relate to body image, your sense of self-esteem will affect your sexual responses. If you feel guilty about past sexual relationships, if you had an abortion or sexually transmitted disease, then you may believe that you are now being punished for your past sexual indiscretions. You have punished yourself enough, it is time to accept that and move on.

If a woman is not relaxed, if she is tense, nervous or apprehensive, if she is distracted by unfamiliar surroundings or unpleasant noises, she may find it difficult to reach orgasm.

For many women intimacy is essential. She wants to be in a loving, committed, long-term, stable relationship where the trust level is high. This kind of woman needs to know that her partner will be there for her on Monday as well as Saturday night.

However, other women find orgasm easier in a new, exciting, different relationship with an element of risk. This is a real turn-on for her.

And there are women who just don't know how, and they have never given themselves permission to experiment and experience.

It is totally unrealistic to expect males to intuitively know exactly what moves will bring every woman to orgasm. Now, if men don't know, and women don't know, it will be pure blind luck if it happens.

Your Relationship

There are the other psychological blocks to reaching orgasm, namely your relationship with your partner. So, please be sure to read Chapter 2 (page 21) of this book. If you are not feeling good about your relationship, if you are unable to communicate openly and honestly about your feelings and know that you will be heard, understood and accepted, then you may have to go back and regain that intimacy that will help you overcome these blocks. Only then can you thoroughly enjoy your sexuality.

Tips to Help You Reach Orgasm

If you are serious about wanting to reach orgasm, then there are a few things that you *must* do for yourself.

For some women, this is the biggest hurdle of all, simply because of the way we were socialized as females. As I've said, women have been taught that nice girls do not look at their genitals, and nice girls certainly do not touch their genitals. Women were told that you will "hurt yourself" or that you will "get an infection" or that "you will not be a virgin any more," and "no man will want you."

You might remember the anguish of the first time you tried to insert a tampon? You did not know where it went, so perhaps you used a mirror to "sneak a peek," then you fumbled around and fooled around till you got it half-way in and half-way out and it was agony. You thought you were going to die. That did not happen, but you still wondered if you were normal. Would you be able to "do it"?

The truth is that nice girls do use tampons and they

do touch their genitals and they even enjoy doing that. They even bring themselves to orgasm. It is essential that you read the section on "Masturbation" (see page 95) and go through the steps described there.

Besides the things you can do for yourself, alone, there are also ways you and your partner can help you reach orgasm.

Number one on your list of priorities is to make time—long, slow, leisurely time with no interruptions, away from phone calls from your mother or from the baby crying. Be sure you have a comfortable setting. Fantasize what you would like; then make it happen: romantic music, ambiance, soft music, candlelight and perhaps a glass of wine. Even if you don't reach orgasm, it will be a night to remember.

Begin with a back massage that is reciprocated. Gradually move on to what I call the "courtship procedure," unchanged over generations and still exciting: kissing gently, then on to necking which is a little more passionate, then French kissing (open mouth kissing). Gradually move on to petting on top of clothing, then petting under clothing and on to genital petting. Be sure you read the section on oral-genital sexual contact (see Chapter 5, page 85). And don't forget to enjoy a sexual fantasy to enhance your pleasure.

It is quite permissible to indicate what you think would be pleasurable for you and also feel free to stimulate your own genitals at the same time. Remember what you learned from your masturbation experiences and incorporate that into arousal with your partner.

Not Every Time

Do remember that you are not likely to have an

orgasm every time you have sex. As Dr. Sol Gordon says, "Not every meal is going to be a gourmet delight; once in a while you are going to dine at a greasy-spoon restaurant." Sex can still be warm, loving and intimate, without being earth shattering. It might even make you appreciate orgasm all the more.

If you and your partner understand this, then you will never again hear "Didja cum?" or "Was it good for you?" Wouldn't it be nice for both of you if we remove all the performance pressure and anxiety? Relax and enjoy.

Faking orgasm, a mistake some men and women make, never helps. In fact, it can only make things worse:

Dear Sue,
For the first eight months of our relationship, I felt I had to "produce" for him, so I faked orgasm. I finally gained confidence to tell him and he was devastated.

There are many, many reasons why females (and males too) fake it. Sometimes in a new relationship where the trust level is not that high and the communication skills are not well established, and the risks of failure are too great, people may act out the most convincing orgasm, complete with movements and sound effects. Males want the new partner to be convinced that he is the greatest lover. Females do not want to wound his ego by telling him how to "do it" better, nor do they want him to think that they are too experienced and have "done it" so often with so many different partners. So they fake it, convinced it will be better next time.

Other times, women try desperately to hold a relationship together. Everything else is coming unglued, but they believe if the sex is still great, maybe they can cement it together again. Or when sex isn't working, she may be terrified he will diagnose her as "frigid" and give up on their sexual relationship. So she fakes it.

Other women regard orgasm as a "gift" you give your partner—something you do to prove how great he is. Perhaps if he is experiencing some sexual dysfunction, and you want to convince him that he is still the greatest, you fake orgasm.

And there are those times when you are really not too enthusiastic about sex, but you feel you should do it to keep him happy and get it over with. You may be exhausted, and he is determined to bring you to orgasm come hell or high water. So you decide to fake it, just so you can finally get some sleep.

Faking it is deceit, plain and simple. And once it becomes a habit, then it is very difficult to go back and say, "Actually I have not had a real orgasm in five years." That can reduce or destroy the trust level in your relationship. If you lied about orgasm, what else have you lied about? It can also shatter his self-image.

Much better to be honest, to be able to say, "Hey, it is just not working for me this evening. I'm not sure why, but I am okay. I'm not feeling frustrated." Or you could say, "I need some time to figure out exactly what is going on for me. I may need to go back and reread the book again."

This is being honest and taking full responsibility for your own sexual satisfaction, or the lack of it, and not blaming him or making him feel like a failure. Honesty is the best policy.

If you have been faking it for ages and now you decide on total honesty, you will be in a bit of a quandary. You can very gently say, "It is not as great as it used to be; I am not sure why, but I really want to work on it. And I will need your help."

Sexual Drought

Either one of you may go through a period when nothing seems to "click." It does not mean that good sex is gone forever. Take time to talk about your relationship. Try to pinpoint any unresolved conflict, buried anger and resentment, stress and tension. Together, try and work these through, so the intimacy can be re-established. Remember, during that interim, you can still sexually satisfy yourself, taking the pressure off your partner and the relationship.

Most large cities have a "Preorgasmia Self-Help Group," women who meet about once a week to share experiences and support and learn from each other. The membership fee for such a group is very reasonable and most counsellors find this is the most effective therapy for women. If you think you would benefit from such a group, phone Planned Parenthood in your area for more information or ask your therapist or counsellor.

Trying Too Hard

Before we leave the topic of orgasm, there is one other myth that we need to dispel. The idea that the ultimate of success in sex is for both partners to "come" together. It is called simultaneous orgasm and it is supposed to indicate total togetherness. I call it goal-oriented sex.

Dear Sue,
My girlfriend and I have good sex. I come first then she comes and it is fine, but I think something is missing. I have heard that it is far more exciting if you and your lover come together. We've tried it. I've tried to slow down, and she's tried to speed up. But we both seem to lose it completely. What are we doing wrong?

This couple is not doing anything wrong, but they have become too goal-oriented. They are trying too hard to get it together and in doing so, they have lost the spontaneity.

When you are sexually aroused and approaching orgasm, you are totally focused on your body, your pleasurable sensations. When you reach orgasm, you are totally oblivious of your partner, you just want them to continue what they are doing. If you have to monitor your partner's excitement level and either speed up or slow down, you lose track of yourself. You are doing this for your partner and not for you. Then you can't fully enjoy your own pleasurable sensations.

Also, half of the joy of sex is watching your partner's facial expressions and body reactions while they are having an orgasm. So if you are heavily into your own orgasm, you are missing your partner's and all the personal satisfaction that may bring you.

Relax, let go, surrender to the sensations, stop watching and waiting, monitoring and anticipating. Get out of your head and into your body.

If simultaneous orgasm happens occasionally and by accident, fine and great, but please do not make it your homework for tonight.

Do read any of the books by Dr. Lonnie Barbach:

For Ourselves, For Each Other, and *Shared Intimacies, Pleasures,* and *Erotic Interludes.* The book *Sex for One* by Betty Dodson is excellent too. These inexpensive paperback books are invaluable as reference and refresher sources. Males in particular will enjoy *Male Sexuality* by Dr. Bernie Zilbergeld.

MALE ORGASM

There is one "fact of life" that you just never seem to hear about: the male orgasm. We always hear about female orgasm, and very little about male orgasm. We seem to assume that if a male ejaculates, that is his orgasm. Wrong. Ejaculation and orgasm are not one and the same.

When a male is sexually aroused and masturbates or has intercourse, he will generally ejaculate, and for him that is good, feels great, the pressure is off; he is relaxed and it was good. Male orgasms vary in intensity, but every once in a while, when he is having sex, it will be spectacular, amazing, explosive, total release. That does not happen every single time nor does he want it to happen every time. He would probably "dry up and blow away."

Do females worry if it does not happen for him on a regular basis? Do we ever say to our partners, "Didja cum?" No way. We really do not worry about it, nor do we feel we have failed if it does not happen. If it happens, wonderful, but we do not put pressure on males to have an orgasm every time they have sex.

It would reduce the performance anxiety on both males and females, if we could apply much the same attitude to female orgasm. Both partners do what they can to make it happen, and if it does, fantastic, and if not, well, it was still pleasurable and enjoyable.

Dear Sue,
Once my husband and I relaxed with sex and started having fun with it, having an orgasm was not the "be all and end all," then orgasms started happening all the time. Now we look back and wonder what the fuss was all about.

What more can I say, folks?

CHAPTER 8

HELP!—MALE

● ● ●

PREMATURE EJACULATION: IT'S OVER BEFORE IT BEGINS

> Dear Sue,
> I really love my partner and we both enjoy sex, but recently I cum before she is anywhere near ready. It is very depressing. I feel like an over-eager teenager out of control. What can I do to cool it?

Premature ejaculation is defined as the problem of any male who ejaculates either before intercourse, thirty seconds after intromission or before five or six thrusts of the penis in the vagina. It is also sometimes defined as the inability to delay ejaculation long enough for both partners to achieve sexual satisfaction.

Premature ejaculation may also be called "sexual incompetency," "ejaculatory inadequacy," or simply "rapid ejaculation." None of these terms paint a pretty picture for a male who fears he has this problem. While I dislike the term "premature ejaculation," or PE, it appears to be the most commonly used and the least pejorative.

This is the one sexual dysfunction for which there are very few known medical causes, such as physical or hormonal abnormalities, and no medication or illness can trigger it.

Studies show that many males who suffer from premature ejaculation are passive in their sexual behaviour but have hostile feelings towards women. They fear sexually aggressive or assertive women, and choose distant, cool, reserved, unresponsive, and sexually undemanding women as their partners.

Before going further, I want to suggest looking at PE from a different perspective. Is it possible that this sexual response is normal for some males? Think about it—if a woman reaches orgasm almost immediately after intercourse, do we call hers "premature orgasmia" and suggest therapy? In all probability, her male partner would be flattered and she would feel that she was just the sexiest person around.

In some parts of the world, a male we diagnose as suffering from PE would be regarded as a macho hero, a real stud and everybody would try to match his time. So it seems to be considered a problem primarily in "civilized" first world countries.

Given that information, we can look at premature

ejaculation as a nuisance, but not the end of the world. Unfortunately, most males who are afflicted with this problem are convinced it is terminal. Some resort to strange tactics: using two condoms, counting sheep, thinking of something unpleasant, avoiding looking at their partner or thinking about it, and so on.

Causes of Premature Ejaculation

Generally, PE is established very early in a male's sexual life patterning. When he began masturbating, he probably felt guilty, embarrassed and ashamed, so he did it surreptitiously and always in a hurry before his parents found out. Then, as he experimented with sex as an adolescent, he was always trying to "cop a feel," and if he got lucky he was able to make out, but it was always in a hurry. He had to do it fast before she realized what was happening and stop it because there was seldom good contraception. Believing that if he "pulled out in time" he would avoid pregnancy, he pulled out in a hurry even if it was not in time.

Then, if the young male became involved with a prostitute, sex was either in a back alley or in a car and again in a hurry. Finally, when he enters a stable relationship he is always so horny that he ejaculates before he even gets his zipper undone. After that, he may suffer only periodic episodes of PE, but it is enough to be threatening, and he is always relieved if he is able to "last longer' the next time. Now he is into performance anxiety. He cannot stop himself from "erection watching," monitoring and even timing the amount of time before he ejaculates. Therapists call it "spectatoring." You can see that a major cause of PE is rooted in the male's sexual history.

Another cause of PE may be in the male's relationship with his partner. If his partner does not enjoy sex, he may tend to do it in a hurry to get it over and done with. If there is anger and resentment and if he and his partner are into games such as "tit for tat," then he may want to deny his partner sexual pleasure. So he comes in a hurry before she can really get into enjoying sex. If the male has a long-term, ongoing problem, he may tend to blame his partner and call her a "castrating woman" or a "ball buster." If a male is having an outside affair, he may feel guilty and to avoid those feelings he wants to hurry and get it over with.

Premature ejaculation has a traumatic effect on a male. He may be embarrassed or ashamed, and sometimes afraid that his partner will laugh, or worse, "let our little secret out of the bag." He fears ridicule from his friends.

A male may also feel that he is not a real man, that he is not in control of his body, and that he is inadequate as a lover. He may fear that he will lose his partner, as this letter shows:

Dear Sue,
I have a big problem. Most of the time when my girlfriend and I have sex, I go off just after entry. I am afraid I can't satisfy my girlfriend's needs and that she might leave me. Except for this, we have a good relationship. What can I do?

At best, premature ejaculation lowers a male's self-image. At worst, he may experience a real sense of failure, which could lead to severe depression. The problem will also affect a male's partner.

The Effects of Premature Ejaculation on Partners

Partners are always aware of a male's problem with PE. Nevertheless, the first reaction is not to talk about it, to deny that it is a problem and to carry on as if nothing were unusual. They try to ignore it, but it will not go away. This reduces the intimacy and the trust level between partners. She tries to protect him from reality, as though he couldn't cope with it.

Meanwhile, the only focus in their sexual relationship is "erection watching," and intercourse that lasts for more than two minutes is the goal—forget pleasure and foreplay!

The partner feels she is contributing to the problem so she "cools" it. She does nothing that might stimulate him, and she will not show any arousal or excitement. She may also feel anger that she is being denied the touching, hugging, petting and fondling that contributes to sexual satisfaction, all because he "comes" too soon.

She may feel that he is rejecting her, that he does not care about her and is doing a version of "wham, bam—thank you, ma'am." Her anger and resentment may contribute to the problem: "Hurry up and get it over with. I don't enjoy it anyhow."

Dear Sue,
I have been going with my boyfriend for eight months and we get along great, except he always ejaculates a few seconds after we begin intercourse. Although I know it is not his fault, it is frustrating. Is there something I can do to prolong the pleasure?

You can see that premature ejaculation can have serious negative effects on a relationship, and, if it has

been a longstanding problem, the couple would benefit from individual and couple counseling.

Before males consider therapy, they usually try a
number of do-it-yourself home remedies without success. These attempts range from drinking alcoholic
beverages or using sedatives to reducing sensations by
using elastic bands around the penis to block ejaculation.

Some men try creams to anaesthetize the penis.
These may include brand names such as Maintain or
Detain and Solarcaine. Nupercainal does numb the
penis, but it will also numb your partner's genitals. It
also tastes terrible, makes your mouth numb, and
sometimes gives you an allergic reaction.

Some males masturbate before intercourse to reduce the arousal level and to slow down ejaculation.
Others try to have sex more frequently to reduce the
urgency of their sex drive. Some males, in their frustration, accuse their partner of "cock-teasing," and
anything the partner does he interprets as teasing, including stepping out of a shower nude and grabbing a
towel.

Some men try distracting mechanisms such as biting their lip hard enough to cause pain as a distrac-
tion, or tensing their muscles, squeezing their legs together because that is less conducive to ejaculation.
Others play mind games with themselves, do complicated mathematical problems in their head to eliminate the preoccupation with ejaculation. Some count
sheep—anything!

Even though these attempts are useless, there is
something you can do for yourself. After ejaculation,

you go through a refractory phase when you lose your erection. Young males can have another erection in ten minutes, and that is extended to two hours in males in their thirties, to four hours in males in their forties, and to eight hours in males in their sixties. Knowing this, young males can use their refractory phase to manually stimulate their partner or for oral-genital stimulation to increase the partner's level of sexual arousal so that she is closer to orgasm by the time your erection happens.

For older males whose erection does not recur until many hours later, all is not lost. You can bring your partner to climax by manual masturbation and oral-genital sex.

Therapy for Premature Ejaculation

You do not have to be in a relationship to start therapy for premature ejaculation. All of the strategies and techniques that are included here can be practised alone very successfully. Then, when you are involved in a relationship you will be knowledgeable and able to help yourself, and you can even include your new partner.

Basically, therapy for PE is a "recognition and re-training" process. When a male is sexually aroused, there is a definite pattern: the excitement phase, the plateau phase, and then the ejaculation phase (and the refractory phase). Towards the end of the plateau phase, there is a very brief period of transition, just before the inevitable ejaculation.

A therapist would likely instruct you to become sexu-ally aroused, which is probably easier alone (by solitary masturbation) than with a partner. Pay very close attention to the sensations you are experiencing. Once you are able to identify that transition phase (it may take several practice runs), then you're ready to learn the stop-start therapy. You become aroused, and at transition stage you stop all stimulation, allow your erection to subside, and then restimulate yourself until you get a sense of control.

The squeeze technique is another effective therapy. As soon as you are aware of the tingling sensation, you very, very gently squeeze the head of your penis at the glans until the erection subsides. Some therapists find their clients do better if they gently squeeze the base of the penis. All stimulation stops; you will lose your erection. Savor the sensations. Then you can easily restimulate yourself by fantasizing and masturbating until you have another full erection. Now, all of a sudden you have this euphoric feeling of being in complete control. This can be a real high for most males.

You can repeat this process several times until you feel that you are ready to ejaculate. Then continue with the stimulation to ejaculation and, probably, orgasm. Hey, you did it, on your own time. But you are not "cured" yet. You will need to practise this until you have a sense of being in complete control.

If you have a sexual partner, you can explain the procedure to her, and she can be involved in the arousal. Together, decide on a signal that you will give your partner—touch their arm, simply say "whoa." When you have reached that point and your partner, very gently squeezes either the glans or the base of your penis until you loose the erection. Then, you can be restimulated to another erection.

Now, this is important: you have to focus solely on *you*. You do not wonder or worry about "where your partner is at, what is happening for her". This is for you alone. During this time you do not touch her or stimulate her in any way.

Here, again, the therapist can be instrumental in helping your partner understand that she is there as a concerned, loving, helpful facilitator, not as a lover at this stage.

The therapist will explain that at this point you need to regain that sense of control, and when you can delay ejaculation till you are ready, then and only then can you try intercourse.

You and your partner may find it less stressful if, before you begin, you please her, stimulate her, by touching, hugging and kissing, masturbation or oral-genital sex till she is aroused and achieves orgasm. Then she will be relaxed—not randy—and not feel that your problem is the only thing that matters and all the attention is focused on you and your erection. She will also be well-lubricated and receptive.

There is a prescribed format for sexual intercourse with your partner. Your partner stimulates you to erection, then very slowly, with you on the bottom on your back she will slowly slide over your pelvis and slowly insert your penis into her vagina. In the first few sessions, you will not move, but she will slowly start to move her pelvis, rotate and move up and down.

During this time, you focus on the pleasurable sensations in your genitals. As soon as you become aware of that "pre-ejaculatory sensation," you signal her to stop, and you remain motionless till your erection subsides. You may find that this is more difficult, and you may need to "go back to square one," solo for a little while, and then progress slowly to this point again.

Once you are able to ejaculate "on your command," then and only then do you proceed with intercourse with you on top. This is the most difficult for most males, because they often have difficulty maintaining control during active thrusting.

So you really have to concentrate, and as soon as you become aware of the pre-ejaculatory sensations, you must stop, allow your erection to subside and then restart. Continue this way until you are ready to ejaculate.

Then you "come" when *you* are ready. There may be relapses, but you now have the skills to regain control.

Help for Your Partner

Along with the changing dynamics resulting from your therapy and the eventual outcome, the other benefit from therapy is that it gives your partner ample opportunity to talk about her feelings about the relationship.

The therapist will help you focus on your feelings and learn to talk about them, probably for the first time, and to re-establish that sense of intimacy that may have been lost.

As therapy progresses, many partners experience feelings of anger and resentment at the amount of attention being devoted to "his problem." The PE may be eliminated, but the underlying relationship problems may really surface and threaten to scuttle your progress. You will need to solve problems as you go along.

Many women feel the progress is not fast enough; it seems to take forever. She may feel as though she is "being used as a sex surrogate," not a loving partner in a relationship of equals. Your partner may feel uncomfortable about you spending so much time in solitary sex, and she may be afraid that you will become "attached to your own right hand" and there will be no need for her in your new found sex life. She may also fear that she "can't get it right," that she is impeding your progress, it is all her fault, and perhaps you would be better off alone. Here, again the therapist needs to be aware of your partner's feelings so you can work it out together to allay her fears.

She may simply give up, unless she is really committed to the therapy and making the relationship work again. She may become disinterested; she may find the therapy tedious and boring. She may complain of fatigue or find other excuses not to be involved.

Think of it as a learning, sharing and growing experience for both of you and an investment in a good, strong, loving relationship with lots of good successful sex.

Premature ejaculation is one sexual dysfunction that responds well to therapy. Although it may take some time, once the therapist has taught you the techniques, you can practise them on your own on a consistent basis. The more you practise, the faster your progress will be. And you will not "wear yourself out." Once you get on a roll, you will actually find yourself enjoying it.

Impotency: I Can't Get It Up

Impotency—the word alone strikes fear into the heart of every male. It threatens his self-image, his sense of himself as a male. At best, he may feel neutered; he may even feel he is now feminine and a wimp, completely ineffectual.

These feelings are reinforced when he hears impotency described as "impaired potency" or "erectile dysfunction."

Impotency is defined as the inability to have and maintain erections sufficient for vaginal penetration and completion of the sex act. Some therapists have qualified it by adding that a male must "last" for seven to eight thrusts, or ten seconds.

Until recently, doctors and therapists maintained that the cause of "impotency was between his ears." In other words, it was purely psychological. We now know the causes are many and varied.

A young male thinks he has this "every-ready penis" and is convinced that it will never go down, and it will last forever. It is a rude awakening the first time his penis lets him down, and he panics and dreads it happening again. It almost becomes a self-fulfilling prophecy: he anticipates it happening, he is anxious, nervous and scared. And so it happens again.

Dear Sue,
I met a girl at university and after a night of dancing we went back to her room. We decided to have sex, only I did not have a condom. By the time she found one, I had lost my erection. We tried everything to get it up again but nothing worked. The situation was

*really embarrassing and I don't want it ever to hap-
pen again. Is it likely to be a problem in the future?*

Now he is convinced he is "losing it." He starts erec-
tion-watching, and monitors its size and shape and
rigidity and how long he can "keep it up." In the
agony of performance anxiety, all pleasure for both
partners is lost. He feels inadequate, frustrated, threatened and cheated.

For help in dealing with these feelings and communicating with your partner, please reread Chapters 2
and 5 on "Relationships," "Communication," "Fantasy,"
"Masturbation" and "Touch." This will take a lot of
pressure off both of you and help you realize that all is
not lost.

Psychological Causes of Impotency

Here are some psychological blocks that can make
men impotent:

• Guilt, sometimes because of an outside "affair" especially if the male was potent in that sexual experience, or because the male has been unable to impregnate his partner.

• Anger, resentment, hostility. ("You bitch, you blew
the budget on that new dress and I'll be damned if I
am going to let you think you can use sex to manipu-
late me," or "I am going to punish you by not giving
you sex.")

• The war of the sexes, an angry reaction against
feminism.

• Hidden aggression, becoming manipulative instead of being openly hostile.

• Trying to do "it" just to prove you can or just to

keep in shape.

• Fear of disease, especially during a sexual encounter with a new partner, or if you have had an outside relationship and you are afraid you might have contracted a disease and might give it to your steady partner.

• Fear of unplanned pregnancy, especially if your method of contraception is not reliable or if you suspect your partner might try to become pregnant to "hook" you into marriage.

• Fear of being forced to marry, as a result of a parental injunction that if you have sex with a female you must marry her.

• Fear of your penis becoming trapped in the vagina during sex or that the female will emasculate you.

• Fear of rejection.

• Stress from job loss, divorce, a family death, a move to a new job or city, bankruptcy. There's that belief: "Success in the boardroom leads to success in the bedroom," and vice versa.

• Unrealistic expectations of a new partner.

• Retirement. You looked forward for years to freedom, being your own boss, energy to indulge in sex, especially "nooners," and quickies. Then when the time comes, you can't perform.

• Conflict with your partner, adolescent kids, your mother-in-law, your boss or your aging parents.

• Basic dislike of sex and your own body or a dislike of your partner's body because of obesity, odours or a pregnancy.

• Partner displays lack of interest.

• A sense of being powerless and not in control of your life.

Physiological Causes of Impotency

There are many organic causes of impotency that are physiological, rather than psychological:

• Medications, which can affect the autonomic nervous system or the circulatory system. Some prescribed medications that may do this are tranquillizers, mood elevators, barbiturates, some medications for colds, diuretics, high blood pressure medications, some drugs used in the treatment of AIDS. If you are on any of these medications and are experiencing impotency, check with your doctor to find out if there are any other medications that could be substituted.

• Any systemic medical diseases such as renal failure, cirrhosis of the liver, asthma or a thyroid disorder.

• Non-prescription drugs such as marijuana and other street drugs.

• Alcohol, thought to be the great disinhibitor, may give you the feeling that you can "do anything, all night long." In reality, it will probably let you down. The old expression, "One drink and you can do anything, three drinks and you can't do a thing" really holds true.

• Stress or exhaustion because your body responds by taking the pressure off and conserving energy by "shutting down" on sexual responses.

• Spinal cord injury, though depending on the seriousness of the condition a male may experience "reflex erections" but they are not the result of sexual stimulation and do not last long enough for intercourse.

• Surgery that involves any of the reproductive organs, most notably prostatic surgery.

• Untreated prostatitis, resulting in inflammation

and infection of the prostate gland. (Treatment with antibiotics is essential.)

• Any vascular disorder or disease. The blood flow to the penis is insufficient, so that it may not become rigid enough to hold an erection. Or, there may be a full erection, but because of a "venous leak" the blood will not remain in the penis long enough for penetration.

• Cigarette smoking reduces the blood supply to the penis.

• Age. In the United States, it is estimated, that twenty percent of males have an erectile dysfunction by age sixty, and by age ninety over eighty percent are affected. We have all heard, "It now takes me all night to do what I used to be doing all night." As males age, the urge to have sexual intercourse is reduced; it takes longer and more stimulation to produce an erection, and it will not be as firm nor will there be the urgency to ejaculate. But regardless of age, he still desires hugging, cuddling, touching, stroking and petting—all the good stuff.

• Diabetes.

• Heart conditions, along with their prescribed medications, and fear of dying or further damaging the heart during sexual excitement and activity. Many times, your partner may also fear the excitement might cause another attack. Most doctors will tell you, if you can climb a single flight of stairs without distress, sex is safe. But they will also warn you not to be involved in a new, very exciting, stimulating sexual relationship with a new partner.

If a male has morning erections—erections during REM sleep—or if he has erections and masturbates successfully, the impotency is generally regarded as psychogenic and would respond to couple counselling and sex therapy. Otherwise, you would be wise to consult a physician to pinpoint the cause of the condition. Incidentally, a word of warning—it is not a great idea to try and have intercourse when an early morning erection occurs after dreaming in REM sleep. The erection will usually disappear as soon as the dreamer is fully awake. Equally unsatisfactory erections may happen in the morning because of a full bladder—what's called a "piss-hard."

Diagnosis of Impotency

To make a diagnosis, your family physician must take an extensive history, focusing on the age of onset, the frequency and situations that seem to trigger impotency, and its effect on your sense of self and on your relationship to your partner. The doctor then does a complete physical exam, including blood pressure, a urinalysis for bladder infections, diabetes and blood tests for hormone levels. The doctor will also ask you if you smoke.

You may think it humorous, but the doctor may suggest you purchase a strip of postage stamps, and when you go to bed, you wrap them around your penis, and seal the two ends together. If you have night erections, the stamps will tear along the perforations. Tell that to your friends and it will get a few laughs. "Rip a strip."

At this point, your doctor may refer you to a urologist, a doctor who specializes in the male reproductive system, or to a sex therapist. Do not be surprised if it takes up to two months to get an appointment. While you wait for your appointment, use that time to do some relationship repair work if necessary. (See the section on "Relationships"—Chapter 2, page 21.) It is also a good time to read a few books on human sexuality. See the bibliography at the end of this book.

Medical Treatment for Impotency

Unfortunately, the old saying "If you don't use it, you lose it," appears to be true. In that case, the best advice is "Never let your meat loaf." If impotency is long-standing or caused by physiological problems, your doctor may prescribe certain drugs. Yohimbine is a drug that causes an increase of blood flowing to the penis and a decrease in the outflow, which results in an erection. It can be taken orally.

This drug has a few negative side effects: it may cause sweating, nausea and vomiting and is not recommended for psychiatric patients, patients with high anxiety or anyone with kidney disease. It is effective for diabetics and some patients suffering from heart disease, but for some people there are no positive effects.

Papaverine combined with pentalomine injections is a smooth muscle relaxant that allows more blood to flow to the penis, which equals bigger, rigid erections. The male is taught exactly how to inject this drug directly into the spongy tissue near the base of the penis, a procedure that strikes fear into the heart of many males but that is quite successful.

The drug is injected ten to twenty minutes before sexual intercourse. The resulting erection may last anywhere from one-half hour to three hours. This treatment, while not recommended for heart disease patients, may be successful for impotency caused by diabetes, prescription drugs, aging, psychological conditions and certain vascular diseases.

The major disadvantage of this drug is that it is possible (though it happens rarely) that the erection will not subside. In that case, the blood in the penis becomes static and does not circulate, so no food and oxygen can nourish it and the tissues may become permanently damaged.

Males using papaverine are warned that if the erection does not go down in a few hours they must go to the emergency unit of the local hospital. The blood will be drained mechanically to prevent permanent damage. Many doctors are now prescribing a new drug—prostaglandins E, which has fewer side effects and involves less chance of a dangerous, prolonged erection.

Implant: Penile Prosthesis

There are three types of penile implants. Basically, they all work the same way. They are surgically implanted into the spongy tissue of the penis, and they remain there.

Semi-rigid implants are a silicone rod, soft and flexible, that provide enough rigidity for intercourse. They make the penis look larger, fleshier and a little longer. Because they are flexible, the penis hangs normally, either erect or flaccid. So, you are not in the guys' locker-room at the golf club with an enviable erection.

Even so, there will be an increase in bulk, and therefore a more noticeable bulge in your trousers, which may result in some odd looks and a bit of teasing from your buddies. If you are up to that, then go for it.

Rigid implants are also available, but they are much

less flexible and more obvious and are seldom used today.

These two implants are the most common, the easiest to implant surgically, have a low complications rate and are virtually fool proof. A penis with an implant is always ready, willing and able, so make sure you are. This means that when you were unable to achieve an erection, you had an excuse not to have sex. Once you have an implant, you no longer have this excuse, so your communication skills with your partner need to be excellent. You still have the right to say "no, not tonight" without having it taken as a put-down, a rejection or "You don't love me any more."

There is another implant, the inflatable, which consists of a hollow latex tube, similar to a long party balloon, inserted into the penis, and connected to a thin plastic tube leading from the base or bottom end to a small plastic bulb that is surgically implanted in the groin near the top of the testicle. This bulb is filled with water, and when you wish to have an erection, you squeeze the bulb several times, forcing the water into the "balloon" in the penis. A mechanical valve shuts and traps the water. Voila, you have your erection. When the erection is no longer needed, you release the valve and the water drains into the bulb, ready for next time.

The advantages of this implant are that you do not have a continual "semi hard-on" all the time, and it appears more natural. The disadvantage is that it is a mechanical device and is therefore subject to failure and break-downs. Getting it fixed is not like taking your car to the garage for repairs. You have to go to the hospital —you are admitted, you go through the preparation for surgery with a general anaesthetic and, usually, the whole unit is replaced.

Penile implants are safe and effective. They may be recommended for impotence that has a physical cause but not to overcome psychological or relationship problems.

Vacuum-Constrictor Devices

For many males who are impotent because of poor circulation, nerve impairment, diabetes, paralysis or other physical disabilities, a new mechanical suction device is now available.

I must admit, it certainly is not romantic and takes the spontaneity out of love making. But if you and your partner can overcome the aesthetics, it is very effective.

The device is a long, hollow, plastic tube, about five centimetres in diameter, open at one end, which is connected by some tubing to a mechanical hand pump. The male inserts his flaccid (non-erect) penis into the tube, right down to the base of the penis. Then he squeezes the pump, which withdraws the air out of the tube. The negative pressure draws blood into the spongy tissue of the penis to produce an erection. A rubber ring slides off the tube and down over the base of the penis to trap the blood and results in an impressive erection.

This device has a gauge to indicate how much suction is there. It should not exceed the recommended limit or you could cause extensive tissue damage. This ring should not be left on for more than five to eight minutes. When you remove it, the erection subsides, and normal circulation returns.

The device costs about $350, and I strongly recommend that you have a doctor or trained expert teach you how to use it properly.

Similar devices have been advertised in many popular men's magazines, promising increased penis size and never ending erections. Unfortunately, they are not well-made and many do not have a safety gauge. The instructions, while enticing, are all too often not complete or specific enough.

One approved device is called "ErecAid" and is successful if both partners overcome their inhibitions. The device can become a pleasurable and romantic part of foreplay, not something the man retreats to the bathroom to do.

Revascularization Surgery

Males who have severe circulatory dysfunctions or insufficiency may benefit from surgery to correct either the venous incompetency or the arterial insufficiency.

This surgery is performed by a specialist in a hospital under a general anaesthetic and requires post-operative time and care. By transplanting either veins or arteries, the blood supply to and from the penis is improved and the patient is able to have full erections.

The procedure does work, and if you are interested, discuss it with your family physician and ask for a referral to a specialist for consultation and testing.

Therapy for Impotency

Unfortunately, our society equates masculinity with the ability to have intercourse and procreate. Consequently, the male's self-image is damaged if he is impotent and he feels less than a man. He may be reluctant to try intercourse again, fearing rejection and ridicule.

Whether the male sexual dysfunction has a physical or psychological cause, there will be stress, so the prime focus of therapy is to remove the performance anxiety. You can do much of it yourself without the guidance of a therapist, provided that the relationship is good, the communications are open and honest, and the love and trust and commitment are there.

In the beginning, we have to eradicate three main myths that can block therapy:

• If a man does not have an erection, it must mean that he is not enjoying the touching, hugging, and petting. Not true. And what's more, most males who are impotent with a partner still have full erections and can enjoy masturbation by themselves.

• It is essential to have sexual intercourse, penis in vagina, for the female to have a grand and glorious orgasm. Again, not true. Most women reach orgasm from clitoral stimulation, and the most effective way is by manual stimulation, or oral-genital sex. No penis involved.

Now, we do have to be honest: a woman does experience a pleasurable sensation from an erect penis thrusting in and out of the vagina. There is a feeling of fullness and containment that is pleasurable, no question. And most females are flattered if their partner has a magnificent erection during the "arousal" phase. They interpret this as meaning "Boy, I can still get him really turned on" and "I am attractive, appealing and interesting." This ego stroking can be achieved in other ways, a simple, "Wow, looking good," can confirm that she is the greatest.

• If a male loses his initial erection, that means he's turned off and it's game over for the night. Wrong! Erections vary—a strong erection may become softer and then return with vigour.

Before beginning therapy, you need to have a medical work-up and verify that there are no physiological reasons why sex "ain't what it used to be" or why it is just not working. Then you move on to sex therapy and relationship counselling.

It is essential that you find a good, qualified therapist whom you like and trust. The therapist is trained to identify problem areas and help you develop the skills to solve your problems. A therapist will also give you accurate information, homework strategies and reading lists.

Please read the section on "Sensate Focus", (Chapter 5, page 108), and then you and your partner can read it together, aloud, and practise. You will both be sexually aroused, but you are to abstain from sexual intercourse, absolutely and no excuses, because that will scupper the whole plan. He will have an erection, she must stop stimulating him, the erection will subside, then she can re-stimulate him.

During the course of your therapy, you and your partner need to explore what your expectations about potency are. If you have blamed all the problems in your relationship on impotency and expect these to magically vanish, you are being unrealistic. Impotency may simply be a symptom of underlying problems. And if the function improves and the problems remain or even increase, he may feel he went through all that and then he never gets to use it.

If partners are angry and resentful, they may unconsciously sabotage the therapy because they have a vested interest in the dysfunction, namely, to have control over their partner.

RETARDED EJACULATION: NOTHING HAPPENS

Retarded ejaculation or, as most male sufferers call it "slow to come," is also called inhibited male orgasm or ejaculatory incompetence.

Retarded ejaculation (RE) is defined as the delay or absence of ejaculation, even after considerable sexual stimulation. He is interested in sex, becomes sexually aroused, has firm erections but is unable to ejaculate and reach orgasm.

Primary RE indicates that a male has never ejaculated or reached orgasm in his life, or has never experienced ejaculation or orgasm with a partner. Secondary RE occurs when a male has functioned satisfactorily in the past, but some trauma or crisis has triggered his inability to ejaculate. Most of these males can masturbate and, if alone, will ejaculate and reach orgasm, but they are unable to do so in the presence of a partner.

In some cases, there may be a smaller amount of ejaculation. Dr. Helen Singer Kaplan, in her book *The New Sex Therapy*, defines retarded ejaculation as the condition of males who become aroused but do not ejaculate in spurts. Instead, the semen drizzles out of the penis and the male does not experience the pleasure and satisfaction of strong muscular contractions and a powerful "shooting" sensation.

Many males try a variety of home remedies with no success. They try drinking too much alcohol in an attempt to relax and "let go." They try pornography to increase arousal levels, along with frequent sex to "keep the system clear." At the other extreme, they try to abstain from sex for long periods of time to become super-charged. Some males try a variety of sexual practices, including some that are abusive. If they think that their partner is holding them back, some try sex with strangers or prostitutes. However, retarded ejaculation is not that easily resolved.

Physiological Causes of Retarded Ejaculation

There are a few physical causes of retarded ejaculation.

- Surgery, such as a prostatectomy.
- Spinal cord injury.
- Nerve disorders.
- Drugs and medications such as narcotics, tranquillizers, hormones and sedatives.
- Aging.
- An enlarged prostate gland.
- Peyronie's disease, a condition that causes the penis to curve and makes sex and ejaculation uncomfortable.
- A blockage or stricture in the urethra. This happens only in rare cases.

Psychological Causes of Retarded Ejaculation

Dear Sue,
I am a normal, healthy, twenty-six-year-old male in a great, loving relationship. I get turned on and have a

magnificent erection, but no matter what I do, no matter what my partner does, I just can't come. I do fine all by myself and it is good, but with my partner, no way.

Retarded ejaculation is generally psychogenic in origin. As the above letter illustrates, most men are quite sexually competent when masturbating. The inhibition arises, in part, from the presence of a partner. As with many other sexual dysfunctions, fear is the basic cause. Many males may be afraid of the following:

• Female genitals or getting lost or trapped in the moist, dark depths of the vagina.

• Hurting themselves or hurting their partner, should they "get carried away."

• Infertility from loss of semen.

• Vigorous thrusting and explosive ejaculation.

• Losing control or becoming addicted to sex.

• Contraceptive failure and unplanned pregnancy.

• Contracting STDs or AIDS.

• Guilt, belief that sex "should" be for procreation only, not for pleasure.

We cannot overlook one major—and very common—cause of delayed ejaculation: your relationship with your partner. If any of the following attitudes influence you and your partner, you may need to get some counselling:

• "Withholding," being determined not to give your partner the satisfaction of knowing that she was able to please and satisfy you.

• Punishing your partner for anything from not taking the garbage out to suspicions that your partner might be having an affair.

• Feeling ambivalence or even revulsion for the partner.

• Adhering to a strict religious upbringing that implies pleasure and satisfaction is sin. "If it is fun, then it must be wrong."

Therapy for Retarded Ejaculation

Therapy for retarded ejaculation is most effective if you have a therapist to help you. The therapy would include:

• Counselling to explore the cause of your fears and anxieties.

• Counselling with your partner to help resolve relationship conflicts, to improve communication and to restore trust and intimacy.

• Establishing the communication level so you do not feel you "should" ejaculate to keep your partner happy.

• Reassuring your partner that this is your problem, that she is not a failure as a lover, that you will not die if you do not ejaculate, and that she is not being replaced by solitary masturbation.

As with other sexual dysfunctions, both male and female, when the performance pressure is lifted and the anxiety is reduced, in all probability the partners can get back on track with great gusto.

OUCH: PAINFUL SEX

Though the percentage of women suffering from dyspareunia (chronic, painful sex) is higher, men also suffer from painful sex. But you seldom hear males talk about it. In fact, you seldom hear males talk about any sexual concerns or dysfunctions. It is not seen as "masculine" to acknowledge that all is not running smoothly in the sexual realm, so you never hear "Sex is a pain" or "Sex hurts." But it can and does happen.

Generally, the discomfort or pain does not begin until a male has a full erection, or until he attempts intercourse, or he is actively thrusting. It is very disconcerting for a male to have to stop everything and explain that he just can't go on, it hurts. This does not fit into the image of what is masculine. So he unconsciously chooses to avoid sexual contact. That seems easier than sitting down with his partner and talking about it.

Because the partner is unaware of the real reason for his avoidance, she internalizes it and takes it personally, which has a damaging effect on the relationship.

Finding the Cause

As with all sexual dysfunctions, it is essential to have a physical examination by your family physician to investigate the cause. The doctor will check for the following physical causes:

• Undiagnosed prostatitis, which causes pain during arousal and ejaculation.

• Tight foreskin, which does not slide easily over the head of the penis during intercourse, causing a "stretching" pain.

• Curvature of the penis, either chordee or Peyronie's disease.

• Previous surgery on any area of the genitals.

• Any STD such as herpes, venereal warts, yeast.

- Problems such as eczema, "jock itch" or infected hair follicles on the penis.
- Epididymitis or infection of the testicles.
- Inguinal hernia, a small section of bowel protruding down and being pinched by the inguinal canal.
- Variocele or rectocele, varicose veins of the testicles.
- Torsion, a twisting of the spermatic cord in the testes.
- Previous negative sexual experiences, such as sexual assault.

Psychological Causes of Painful Sex in Males

When the family doctor has ruled out physical causes, he may explore with you possible psychological causes or he may refer you to a therapist. There are many psychological causes such as the following:

- Guilt, shame, embarrassment, ignorance or misinformation.
- Anger, resentment or hostility in the relationship.
- Feeling pressured into sex against your will and having the sense that you are not "in control" of your sexual relationship.
- Fear of unplanned pregnancy.
- Fear of STDs or AIDS.
- Fear of "trapped penis" or emasculation by the female.
- Fear of hurting your partner.
- Being turned off by your partner.
- Another relationship on the side. Generally the pain occurs only during sex with regular partner, not with the outside lover.

Regardless of the cause of a male's dyspareunia, his partner may react negatively unless they can communicate about it, openly and honestly, without accusing or laying blame or applying liberal doses of guilt. She may have a variety of responses to his problem:

• She may lose respect for her partner and see him as "not all man."

• She may become suspicious: "Is he getting it somewhere else?" or "Is he gay and has not told me?"

• "He does not love me any more" or "He does not find me appealing and sexy any more."

• "We will never be able to have a baby."

To prevent or reduce the spiralling disintegration of the relationship, a man must get counselling as soon as possible. He and his partner must start communicating their feelings and their love and concern. I strongly recommend that both partners begin keeping a journal, so you are aware of your feelings and the dynamics of the relationship.

A therapist would likely recommend that you take the pressure off sex by agreeing to avoid sexual intercourse. You can "do everything but . . ." and emphasize sensate focus, mutual masturbation, unless that causes pain for him, and he can always bring his partner to orgasm by masturbation or oral-genital sex.

The success rate of sex therapy for dyspareunia is very high, and the amount of therapy time is quite low. Once the couple have insight into the cause and have the communications back on track, improvement is rapid and permanent.

So don't put it off. Get moving on a medical checkup and counselling as soon as possible.

CHAPTER 9

HELP!—FEMALE

• • •

DYSPAREUNIA: PAIN DURING INTERCOURSE

Dear Sue,
I love my boyfriend and I love touching, petting and
oral sex. But when it comes to going all the way, forget
it—it hurts. I want to enjoy sex, but every time his
penis is near me, I get scared that it will hurt and I
push him away. He does not pressure me, but I am
afraid we will break up if I don't get over this.

Dyspareunia is simply painful sex that persists over a
period of time. "Painful sex" is almost a contradiction
in terms. Sex is supposed to be a spontaneous pleasure and the height of a joyful intimacy. Pain does not
fit into this scenario.

Psychological and Physical Causes of Dyspareunia

There are many women who experience physical pain during sexual activity and intercourse. It is usually sporadic, occasional or cyclic and may have any of the following causes:

- Stress or anxiety.
- Fear of unplanned pregnancy.
- Fear of STDs or AIDS.
- Ovarian cysts, endometriosis or adhesions from surgery.
- A tipped uterus or retroversion.
- Aging, drying and thinning of the vaginal walls.
- Premenstrual syndrome.
- Constipation, impacted feces or hemorrhoids.
- Previous negative sexual experiences, such as sexual assault or incest.
- Tight or resistant hymen.
- Insufficient arousal and insufficient lubrication.
- Deep thrusting or sexual activity that is too vigorous.
- Not wanting to have sex.
- Anger, resentment or poor communication in the relationship.
- Fear of pain.

Many of these causes can be temporary and do not have negative effects on the sexual relationship. But if the pain becomes chronic, and you come to anticipate pain every time you have sex, you will consciously or unconsciously avoid sex, especially intercourse. This is classed as dyspareunia.

Some gynaecologists say that dyspareunia makes up about eighteen to twenty percent of the reasons for consultations for sexual difficulties. When you visit your family doctor because of painful sex, you will gain more from the consultation if you are able to:

• Pinpoint exactly where the pain is located, and describe whether it radiates to other areas.

• Describe exactly what the pain is like, whether it is sharp, burning, etc.

• Describe whether the pain increases in certain positions.

• Detect whether the pain corresponds with menstrual cycles or other specific times such as weekends.

• Give the date of your last menstrual period.

• Give the date(s) of any major surgery.

• Detect whether the pain is preceded by stress, quarrels, grief, anger or other upsets.

• Describe what your feelings are when you have sex, whether you are in the mood, feeling loving, receptive, and sexually responsive.

• Describe the extent of genital lubrication.

• Talk about your fears—whether you are afraid of an unplanned pregnancy, contracting STDs or AIDS.

• Detect whether you are menopausal or pre-menopausal.

• Remember whether sex has always hurt, or when it began to be painful and whether it is becoming worse.

• Consider whether the pain could be related to incest or sexual assault.

Your family physician will take a full history and conduct a physical examination, including a pelvic examination. The doctor will check for any signs of vaginal infection such as yeast, warts, chlamydia, or herpes. He or she will also look for cervical erosions, and will take a pap smear and culture for gonorrhea. Then a bimanual exam will follow. The doctor, wearing a glove, will gently insert two fingers into the vagina to locate the cervix, and with the other hand outside will press down on the abdomen to feel (palpate) the uterus. This is done to detect tumors or endometriosis. The doctor will also locate the ovaries and check for ovarian cysts. He or she may even request an ultrasound (type of X-ray) to rule out any physical cause for the pain during intercourse.

Treatment of Dyspareunia

Some causes of dyspareunia can be treated medically or surgically. The following are examples:

• Surgery may be recommended for a tipped uterus, which can cause agony during intercourse. During surgery, the uterus is lifted and tilted and supported.

• Yeast, chlamydia, or trichomonas or other vaginal infections can be treated and cured. It may take up to two months before healing is complete.

• Pelvic inflammatory disease (PID) makes sex painful, but is difficult to treat except surgically.

• A hymen partially blocking the vaginal opening results in painful sex, and minor surgery can correct the problem.

• Constipation or impacted feces in the rectum may make intercourse uncomfortable and is easily treated.

Therapy for Dyspareunia

When the doctor has ruled out physical causes for the pain during intercourse, he may suggest you have counselling. Therapy would focus on finding and eliminating the reasons for your avoidance of sexual intercourse. This would include exploring your fears and anxieties as well as finding unconscious reasons.

Dyspareunia might be triggered by a change in the dynamics of your relationship, unresolved conflict, power struggles, and anger or resentment, or even hatred. Generally, a therapist's clue that the problem is based in the relationship comes if a woman says something like "It starts to hurt the minute he comes near me."

The therapist may take you through a series of anxiety-provoking fantasy trips to encourage you to face your fears. As you proceed through the scenarios, you are taught to relax and to realize that your responses are irrational in your situation. Gradually you will learn to deal with these fears so that they no longer control you. The therapist may also use hypnosis, tranquillizers and sedatives, combined with encouragement and reassurance.

Meanwhile, your partner should be encouraged to develop an awareness and understanding of what is happening to you, and might participate in the "homework" of therapy.

You may find it beneficial to keep a journal to jot down your feelings, your moods and your thoughts about what you are experiencing. Don't let worries about punctuation, grammar or spelling stop you from doing it. You may be surprised to find that when you reread your musings, you really gain some insights into what is happening for you.

VAGINISMUS: DON'T COME NEAR ME

Vaginismus is defined as painful sexual intercourse of long-standing. It is a persistent, involuntary spasm of the musculature of the outer one-third of the vagina. The female, anticipating pain during sex, tightens the pubococcygeal muscles. The vaginal opening goes into spasm, which is severe enough to make sexual intercourse impossible.

Without therapeutic intervention, the female, even though she may be sexually aroused, is totally unable to just relax and let sex happen. Generally, the minute the partner comes near her and touches her, the spasms begin and do not stop until he is no longer in the vicinity.

Causes of Vaginismus

As is the case for other sexual dysfunctions, a woman who suffers from vaginismus needs a full physical examination, including a pelvic examination (see section on dyspareunia). If the examination shows no physical dysfunctions, the doctor can refer her to a competent sex therapist.

In most cases, the male partner is a contributing factor in the condition. Many females who experience vaginismus are not knowledgeable about sex, and may have been brought up with a strict religious background that emphasized that "Sex is not for the woman's pleasure, but for procreation only." However, males have these desires which a female must endure to keep the relationship together." Her method of reducing the frequency of sex is to complain of pain. If he insists or is forceful, the vagina goes into spasm to prevent intercourse.

Vaginismus is a common reaction to sexual assault (rape), incest or sexual abuse. These kinds of negative sexual experiences usually result in anger, resentment and rage against all males, even a beloved partner. The penis is seen as a weapon. This is supported by slang terminology such as rod, gun, tool, prod, prick.

Generally, the couple has a low level of intimacy, with difficulty communicating about sexual feelings. Combined with ignorance and misinformation, this contributes to unrealistic expectations of sex. The male may be insensitive to the needs, wants and desires of his partner. There may have been insufficient sexual foreplay and arousal and too much emphasis on intercourse. He may rely heavily on pornography, and his partner, resenting this, will turn off sex, particularly if he enjoys vigorous, forceful, even brutal, violent sex as portrayed in many porn magazines. The women in these magazines are always depicted as enjoying it eventually so he escalates the activity, which aggravates the problem dramatically.

However, other women with a phobia of penile insertion have established a satisfactory sexual relationship relying on mutual masturbation and oral sex to orgasm.

Therapy for Vaginismus
Females can gain some help from sex education books such as *The New Our Bodies, Ourselves* by the Boston Women's Health Collective, and Sheila Kitzinger's book *The Sexual Experiences of Women*. An understanding of male sexuality is also helpful from books such as *Male Sexuality* by Dr. Bernie Zilbergeld and *Private Parts: An Owner's Guide* by Dr. Yosh Taguchi.

Sex therapy for vaginismus may take some time because the causes are deep and ingrained over a long period of time and are well established. The counsellor will need to go back to the immediate cause of the disorder and work through the woman's phobic reactions and responses. The therapist will also want to work on the relationship, so both partners need to participate in individual and joint counselling. As the intimacy, trust and communications improve, the partners can begin non-genital sexual contact—hugging, holding, caressing, massage, sensate focus, but they must abstain from all genital contact.

The couple needs to learn that there is more to sex than a penis in the vagina, and that there is pleasure, joy and satisfaction in other forms of sexual expression. The male can masturbate, either alone, or in her presence, but she is not to be involved at this stage. The therapist will already have taught her how to do Kegel exercises (see page 123), which she can practise.

The female partner will then be encouraged to have a long, luxurious bath to help her relax. Then she will use a magnifying mirror to look at her genitals, to touch her genitals, identify the clitoris, the urethra, the vagina and the anus. Then she may be given a set of soft, plastic, pliable, blunt rods, graduated in size, or she may simply be instructed to begin by using her baby finger. Using lots of lubrication, she very gently, very gradually, she inserts the smallest dilator or her baby finger into the vagina. It may take a week or two before she is ready to proceed further.

When she can do this without discomfort or anxiety, she may progress to the next size dilator or her middle finger. Then she progresses to two fingers or a dilator

of larger diameter; next, three fingers and on to four
fingers.

The therapist will probably suggest that she not proceed any further until she is completely comfortable
and enjoying the sensations of touching her own genitals. Then the therapist may suggest that she purchase
a plastic vibrator or dildo and learn to be comfortable
with that. Next, she learns to masturbate all by herself
and to sexually pleasure and satisfy herself.

At this point, her partner will become involved, just
watching in the beginning, then gently touching her
genitals, and on to oral-genital sex. Then, using lots of
lubrication, he will gently insert his baby finger into
her vagina with no movement—just let it rest till she
gets used to the sensation. Then he may gently move
his finger in and out, slowly and gently.

Once she is comfortable with this he can proceed to
two, three and four fingers. This will take a little time,
but he will be encouraged as she makes progress, and
the intimacy and trust level rises.

The next step is genital-to-genital contact. He masturbates and ejaculates outside her vagina. Then he
will gradually and gently insert his penis into her
vagina after sexual stimulation and arousal, and just
allow it to rest there—no thrusting, just being there.
Gradually they can both participate in intercourse
with the clear understanding that the minute she experiences any anxiety, discomfort or pain, it will stop
and they will take a break to reintegrate, go back to a
point that she is comfortable with and proceed slowly
from there.

Therapy for vaginismus does take time. But think
of it in terms of an investment in time, your sexual

satisfaction, your relationship with your partner and your partner's sexual satisfaction. In that way, it becomes something worth working towards. The relationship will certainly benefit, and both partners will grow and experience a better self-image with stronger communication and a loving, trusting relationship.

Believe me, it is worth it in the end.

CHAPTER 10

HOOKED ON SEX

• • •

SEXUAL ADDICTION

Sexual addiction is a very controversial topic. It is not recognized by the American Psychiatric Association as a sexual dysfunction. It is considered an obsessive or compulsive behaviour, and as such, the Association would not include sexual addiction in this book.

However, as a sex counsellor on radio and TV shows, I am very aware that this is becoming a common concern among males. It is less common, but just as problematic among females. Because it manifests itself differently in women as "love addiction," we will discuss it separately.

Sexual Addiction in Males

> *Dear Sue,*
> *Sex—I just can't get enough. It's not that I want a weekend orgy in the sack, non-stop sex. No, I will meet a lady in a bar, pick her up, have sex, leave and go back to the bar and do it all over again.*

As this letter illustrates, sexual addiction is compulsive, sexual behaviour—not necessarily intercourse—that is generally devoid of personal feelings for the other person. It is sexual activity for relief, comfort, excitement, reassurance or power.

Sexual addiction is more than sexual desire; it is sexual dependency. Males who become obsessed with sex interpret everything with sexual overtones and innuendos and connotations. It is estimated that up to six percent of males are "sex junkies." It is far more common in societies where performance, possessions, money, power and control are emphasized. Sufferers become "hooked" on frequent joyless sexual affairs. They go for quantity rather than quality.

There is a close resemblance between an alcoholic or drug addict and a sex addict. In fact, many sex addicts are also substance abusers. These people appear to be able to distort their life experiences to justify their behaviour. This may be expressed by exhibitionism, voyeurism, sexual assault or multiple partners.

Causes of Sexual Addiction

The causes of sexual addiction are many and varied, but there a few commonalities. Most sufferers, both male and female, were sexually abused as children. Also, they generally suffer from low self-concept/self-esteem, and sex seems to prove their worth as a person. Sex is used to reinforce masculinity and potency in males, when they think they cannot contribute anything else to the relationship.

Both males and females who are sex addicts are basically poor communicators, unable to initiate an intimate relationship nor sustain it. Typically, after an argument, rather than resolving the conflict, the male resorts to sex as a solution, as a pacifier.

Many addicts see sex as a challenge and a conquest, and spend an inordinate amount of time and effort in pursuit of their "pastime," which they regard as harmless sport, fun and games.

Some become addicted to the thrill of the chase, the "high," the "rush," the excitement, and gradually they need more and more of their fix to produce the same high. It energizes and exhilarates.

Sexual addiction may be used as an escape mechanism to avoid painful feelings, closeness or intimacy, and the risk of rejection.

Most sexual addicts are unable to sustain a stable, loving relationship and the trust level is shattered. Although the addict feels guilty and promises to change, the urge is too strong and he falls back into his addiction, regardless of its effect on the partner, children, parents and friends. We are talking about a dependency, which if not indulged in results in the same symptoms of withdrawal as any other addiction—cold turkey suffering.

Sexual addicts become secretive because their behaviour is not acceptable. They lie, they deceive partners and friends. They cannot be trusted and any beginning of a relationship does not last.

Therapy for Sexual Addiction

The most effective therapy is based on the Alcoholics Anonymous credo with its twelve steps to recovery and public recognition and acknowledgement: "My name is Bill and I am a sex addict."

Sex addicts also need counselling for the following:

- To deal with the sexual abuse in their childhood.
- To resolve their feelings of anger and hatred.
- To build up their self-image and to develop feelings of adequacy and competency.
- To help sufferers look at the needs that are being met by their addiction; to decide whether those needs are healthy and essential and, if not, to dump and replace them; to find effective ways to satisfy those needs that are healthy.
- To teach communication skills to help establish and maintain intimate relationships with partner, family and friends.

An inevitable outcome will be a dramatic growth in self-concept and self-esteem, so that you feel you deserve the best and are unwilling to settle for less. If you feel that you might be addicted to sex or love, please make an appointment with a psychologist, psychiatrist or a well-qualified therapist. This is not something you can do for yourself by "pop psychology." On the other hand, there are some excellent "self-help" books that might give you some insight into your addiction and some clues as to possible therapy. See the list of books at the end of the chapter.

SEX ADDICTION IN WOMEN

Women who "couldn't get enough sex" used to be called nymphomaniacs, and it was many men's fantasy to find a "nymph" with an insatiable libido. It was considered to be a disorder caused by a need to prove they were not lesbian or "frigid." Now we know that there are some women who enjoy sex more than others, without the behaviour being dysfunctional. Women also often give sex to get love, but this too is not a true sexual addiction.

For women who are addicted to love or to being in love, *not* being in love is a catastrophe. Love proves their worth. Women who are love addicts often suffer from feelings of depression, failure, inadequacy as a female, anxiety, confusion, irritability and desperation.

Causes of Sex Addiction

Usually females who suffer from love addiction were deprived as children, and now need constant reassurance that they are lovable. As with males, most were physically or sexually abused or victims of incest or early rape. They learned very early to use sex to get what they wanted—a new bicycle, money, new clothes, praise and acceptance in their family.

Usually addicted females have a low self-concept, self-esteem, and the only value they feel they have is as a sex object: "It is the least I can do in return for a nice evening."

The love addict needs the on-going excitement of "being in love"—the thrill of the chase, the excitement, the high. Once "the honeymoon is over," she needs more of the excitement, so she does not work on the old relationship. She moves on rapidly to a "new and exciting love." She may also use the quest for love as a way of preventing or counteracting boredom.

Therapy for Sex Addiction

Therapy for love addicts is very similar to the therapy for sexual addiction that affects males. Women need to learn to be self-sufficient and to live independently without a partner or lover. A therapist helps addicts explore other activities that might bring about the same rewards and positive strokes that the addict got from the frantic search for love.

Therapy for love addiction takes a great deal of time, so you must be prepared to invest considerable time and effort for the therapy to be successful. But the long-term outcome will be a change for the better and have a positive effect on your relationships with your partner and your family.

I recommend you find a psychiatrist or a psychologist and begin therapy to prevent further erosion of your primary relationship. Most cities have a self-help support group listed in the phone book. For more information, check the "Other Resources" section in the appendix.

Here are some good books on the subject: *Escape from Intimacy* by Dr. Anne Schaffen, *Women Who Love Too Much* by Robin Norwood, *Love and Addiction* by Stanton Peel, *Sexual Addiction* by Dr. Patrick Carnes. *Men Who Can't Love*, by Julia Sokol is a good read for women who tend to fall in love with men unwilling to sustain a relationship.

APPENDIX

DON'T JUST SIT THERE, DO SOMETHING—ORGANIZATIONS AND BOOKS

• • •

ORGANIZATIONS THAT CAN HELP

There are many organizations across the country that are designed to help you in a specific problem area. Finding the right one can be difficult, especially if you are in a panic.

Telephone Book

The telephone book can be a great ally, both the Yellow and Blue Pages.

The Blue Pages are divided into three sections located at the back of your regular telephone directory:

Government of Canada, Provincial Government and Municipal (local) government. Here you will find:

• Department of Public Health (local) for information on birth control and STD and AIDS clinics.

• Mental health clinics.

• Family services.

Even if you think that these sources will not be able to help you, they will have a list of other agencies that can. In all probability, they will not recommend private therapists or counsellors.

In the Yellow Pages, you will find a comprehensive list of organizations that can help you, listed under "Social Service Organizations." For example, here you will find your local AIDS committee, a group that is most helpful in referring you to agencies, counselling and support groups.

This section also lists your local Rape Crisis Centre, sometimes also called Sexual Assault Centre. It will likely be listed under your municipality or county name, for example Kitchener-Waterloo Sexual Assault Counselling Centre.

For individual relationship or sex counselling, look in the Yellow Pages index under "Marriage, Family and Individual Counselling." Also in the Yellow Pages index, you will find the heading "Women's Organizations and Services." Look down the list till you find one that you think could help you. An example is Women's Counselling Referral Education Centre (WRECK) in Toronto.

Other Resources

In the United States, one of your best sources of help would be SIECUS (Sex Information and

Education Council of the United States): 130 West 42nd Street, Suite 2500, New York, New York, 10036. A similar organization in Canada is SIECCAN (Sex Information and Education Council of Canada): 850 Coxwell Avenue, East York, Ontario, M4C 5R1.

Or try your local YMCA, YWCA or YMHA. Besides providing exercise programs, the YWCA in many major cities will probably have an "Incest Survivors" group or can refer you to such a group.

Planned Parenthood is another helpful agency. They usually have complete up-to-date files and can give you the information you need. In some areas, they have a clinic and some even provide counselling services. Check it out.

The Salvation Army can be invaluable in helping you locate a hostel for battered women and their children. Here again, in an emergency, don't hesitate to contact your local Police Department. They know where the "safe houses" or women's shelters are and how to get in.

Some smaller towns now have a Community Health Centre with staff who can help you. Also, your family doctor may be able to help you in an emergency, or to refer you to someone who can help. Check them out.

In Toronto, the Public Library has a "Self Help Clearing House," which can refer you to a therapy support group in an area of concern to you. Look up "Self Help Clearing House" in the Toronto telephone directory white pages for information on "self-led" or "leaderless" groups. The fee for these groups is very reasonable because you are not paying for a group leader. Generally, a leader emerges in any group, and the group dynamics prevent them from getting too far off track. These groups are excellent for ongoing therapy after intensive private counselling.

In the United States, the resources are similar to those in Canada. National organizations include AASECT—The American Association of Sex Educators, Counsellors and Therapists—which will provide a list of certified therapists in your area: 435 North Michigan Avenue, Suite 1717, Chicago, Illinois, 60611.

Most large universities in the U.S. are associated with hospitals that have sex therapy clinics which can be accessed through the out-patient department or by referral from a family doctor. For sexual addiction there is the National Association on Sexual Addiction and an in-patient therapy clinic: Golden Valley Health Center, 4101 Golden Valley Road, Golden Valley, Minnesota, 55422. There is also Sex and Love Addicts Anonymous, whose head office is: P.O. Box 119, New Town Branch, Boston, Massachusetts, 02258.

It may take a lot of research and time on the phone to locate service that would be beneficial for you, but stay with it. Good luck in your search.

SUGGESTED BOOKS

Male Sexuality

De Angelis, Barbara. *Secrets about Men Every Woman Should Know.* New York: Delacorte Press, 1990.
Goldberg, Herb. *The Hazards of Being Male.* New York: Signet, 1977.
Goldberg, Herb. *The Inner Male.* Markham, Canada: Signet, 1988.

Goldberg, Herb. *The New Male*. New York: Morrow, 1980.

Hite, Shere. *The Hite Report on Male Sexuality*. New York: Ballantine, 1981.

MacKenzie, Bruce and Eileen. *A Couple's Guide to Overcoming Impotency*. New York: Henry Holt, 1988.

Taguchi, Dr. Yosh. *Private Parts: An Owner's Guide*. New York: Doubleday, 1989.

Zilbergeld, Ph.D., Bernie. *Male Sexuality*. New York: Bantam, 1978.

Female Sexuality

Boston Women's Health Collective. *The New Our Bodies, Ourselves*. New York: Simon & Schuster, 1984.

Hite, Shere. *The Hite Report*. New York: Dell, 1976. (Easy to read; about women's attitudes towards sex and relationships.)

Kitzinger, Dr. Sheila. *Sexual Experiences of Women*. London and New York: Putnam, 1983.

Sex and Aging

Boston Women's Health Collective. *Ourselves Growing Older*. New York: Touchstone Books, Simon & Schuster, 1987.

Butler, Robert, and Myrna Lew. *Love and Sex After Forty—A Guide for Men and Women in their Later Years*. New York: Harper & Row, 1986.

Cobb, Janine O'Leary. *Understanding Menopause*. Toronto: Key Porter Books, 1988.

Greenwood, Sadja. *Menopause Naturally*. New York: Volcano Press, 1989.

Older, Julia. *Endometriosis*. New York: Scribner, 1988.

Rubin, Lillian B. *Women of a Certain Age*. New York: Harper & Row Publishers, 1979.

Wollison, Mary Anne. *Prime Times*. Markham, Canada: Paperjacks, 1987.

Orgasm

Barbach, Ph.D., Lonnie. *For Each Other*. New York: Doubleday Anchor Press, 1984.

Barbach, Ph.D., Lonnie. *For Yourself*. New York: Signet, 1975.

Barbach, Ph.D., Lonnie. *Shared Intimacies*. New York: Perennial Library, 1985.

Comfort, Dr. Alex. *The Joy of Sex*. New York: Crown, 1972.

Dodson, Betty. *Self Love*. New York: self-published, 1985.

Heiman, Julia, and Dr. Joseph Lopiccolo. *Becoming Orgasmic*. New York: Prentice Hall, 1988.

Relationships

Bach, George, and Peter Wyden. *The Intimate Enemy*. New York: Avon, 1970. (How to "fight fair" in a relationship.)

Bach, George, and Ronald Deutsch. *Pairing*. New York: Avon, 1970. (Why you are attracted to one person rather than to another.)

Berne, Eric. *Sex and Human Loving*. New York: Kangaroo, 1975. (Basic understanding of relationships. Old, but still good.)

Blake, Mike. *Human Sexual Relations*. New York: Pantheon, 1988. (A compilation of writing by famous therapists.)

Burns, David. *Intimate Connections.* New York: Signet, 1985. (Self-concept/self-esteem and how to meet potential partners.)

Carter, Stephen, and Julia Sokol. *Men Who Can't Love.* New York: Berkley, 1987. (Written for women who are attracted to men who flee from intimate relationships.)

Clark, Ph.D., Don. *The New Loving Someone Gay.* Berkeley: Fitzhenry & Whiteside, 1990.

Eichenbaun, Louise, and Susie Orba. *Understanding Women—A Feminist Psychoanalytic Approach.* New York: Basic, 1983.

Fast Julius. *Body Language.* New York: Kangaroo, 1970. (About unspoken messages and signals we give with our body.)

Friday, Nancy. *Jealousy.* New York and Toronto: Bantam, 1985.

Hite, Shere. *Good Guys, Bad Guys and Other Lovers—A Guide to Relationships.* New York: Pandora, 1989.

Lerner, Harriet. *The Dance of Anger.* New York: Perennial Library, 1987. (Explains the role of anger in relationships.)

Lerner, Harriet. *The Dance of Intimacy.* New York: Perennial Library, 1987. (About the way women react to relationships.)

Norwood, Robin. *Women Who Love Too Much.* New York: Kangaroo, 1985. (About women who repeatedly become involved in "no-win" relationships.)

Scarf, Maggie. *Intimate Partners.* New York: Ballantine, 1987.

Tschirhart-Sanford, Linda, and Mary Ellen Donovan. *Women and Self-Esteem.* New York: Penguin, 1984. (Explores how self-image affects our lives and loves, and suggestions for improvement.)

Vaughan, Peggy. *The Monogamy Myth*. New York: Fitzhenry & Whiteside, 1989.

Wright, John. *Survival Strategies for Couples*. Toronto: McClelland & Stewart, 1985. (Excellent on techniques to get a good relationship back on track again.)

Fantasy

Barbach, Ph.D., Lonnie. *Erotic Interludes*. New York: Perennial Library, 1986. (A book of sexual fantasies for males and females.)

Barbach, Ph.D., Lonnie. *Pleasures*. New York: Perennial Library, 1984.

Friday, Nancy. *Forbidden Flowers. More Women's Fantasies.* New York: Kangaroo, 1982.

Friday, Nancy. *Men in Lore.* New York: Dell, 1980.

Friday, Nancy. *My Secret Garden.* New York: Kangaroo, 1973.

Sexual Assault and Incest

Barnes, Patty Deerosier. *The Woman Inside—From Victim to Survivor.* Racine, Wisconsin: Mother Courage Press, 1989.

Bass, Ellen, and Laura Davis. *Courage to Heal.* New York: Perennial Library, 1988.

Blume, E. Sue. *Secret Survivors.* New York: John Wiley & Sons, 1990. (Excellent for women who are victims of incest, working towards becoming survivors.)

Los Angeles Commission on Assaults Against Women. *Surviving Sexual Assault.* Los Angeles: Fitzhenry & Whiteside, 1980.

Nicarthy, Ginny, and Sue Davidson. *You Can Be Free.*

Seattle: Seal, 1989.
Stank, Elizabeth. *Intimate Intrusions*. New York: Routledge, Chapman Hall Publishers, 1985.
Warshaw, Robin. *I Never Called It Rape*. New York and San Francisco: Perennial Library, 1988.

Sue Johanson

TALK SEX: SUE TELLS IT LIKE IT IS

With hundreds of teenagers asking for her advice on her TV and radio shows and by letter, in person or by phone, Sue Johanson, "The Sex Lady", decided to write a book addressing the issues most frequently raised by her young fans. With *Talk Sex*, Johanson takes a lively and down-to-earth approach to the sex questions posed her by her teenage audience. Answering such queries as "Do girls ovulate every month?" to "What is an orgasm?" to "Can guys get yeast infections?", Johanson tackles the topics that most kids are too embarrassed to ask their parents about. *Talk Sex* is a must-have for any teen with a question about sex.